IMAGES
of America

JEFFERSON BARRACKS

During several periods in its history, Jefferson Barracks was one of the largest induction centers in the United States. World War II was one of those times. The author's father, Hardy Jack Smith (1922–2010), became one of the myriad citizen soldiers who began his military career at Jefferson Barracks in 1944. (Joseph J. Grassino.)

ON THE COVER: This cover is part of a panoramic photograph of a military formation for review taken at Jefferson Barracks during World War II, sometime after the 1943 construction of the Red Cross building (with four white pillars) in the left background. The original, which measures about 10 inches by 2 feet, is representative of massive panoramic photographs taken to document newly inducted troops or troops preparing to deploy. (Marc Kollbaum.)

IMAGES
of America

JEFFERSON BARRACKS

Sandie Grassino and Maj. (Ret.) Art Schuermann

ARCADIA
PUBLISHING

Published by Arcadia Publishing
Charleston, South Carolina

Printed in the United States of America

Library of Congress Control Number: 2009943863

For all general information, please contact Arcadia Publishing:
Telephone 843-853-2070
Fax 843-853-0044
E-mail sales@arcadiapublishing.com
For customer service and orders:
Toll-Free 1-888-313-2665

Visit us on the Internet at www.arcadiapublishing.com

To my late father, Hardy J. Smith—inducted at Jefferson
Barracks in 1944—and to all the brave who passed
through Jefferson Barracks, creating its history

CONTENTS

FOREWORD

In 1826, Jefferson Barracks was appropriately named to honor Pres. Thomas Jefferson, who died earlier that year. His vision led to the Louisiana Purchase and launched the exploration of the West. Jefferson Barracks remains the oldest US military installation west of the Mississippi that is in continuous use. Today, it stands as a national treasure in the American heartland. Here, our citizen soldiers have trained and served to protect our freedoms for generations. Here, future presidents and generals were shaped early in their careers to become great leaders. Here, the current and future military challenges of our nation are met with America's best and brightest soldiers using state-of-the-art technology. Here, brave soldiers who have fallen in battle or died peacefully at home are laid to rest in the hallowed ground of the national cemetery along with veterans from every conflict since the American Revolution.

I want to give a special thanks to the authors Sandie Grassino and Maj. (Ret.) Art Schuermann for this important work. Also, I want to acknowledge the work of the Jefferson Barracks Community Council, which I helped initiate, that brings together all the assets of Jefferson Barracks and the community to preserve its legacy and promote its future because it is vital to our national security and our local economy.

This book captures in words and images what Jefferson Barracks has meant for the United States and will be a valuable tool for historians, teachers, and families, reminding future generations of how we honor our veterans and serve our country.

Let us never forget that freedom is not free.

—Russ Carnahan
US Representative
Missouri Third Congressional District

ACKNOWLEDGMENTS

We wish to extend special thanks to the following for their generous help and immense knowledge contributed toward this work: the Carondelet Historical Society; Bill Florich; the Friends of Jefferson Barracks; the Gettysburg National Military Park Museum; Joseph J. Grassino; the Heritage Foundation of Jefferson Barracks; Micaela Gilchrist; Debbie Stinson Hull; Kenerly Family History and Kedrick Kenerly; the Knight Family Archives; Marc Kollbaum and St. Louis County Department of Parks and Recreation; the Library of Congress (credited as LOC); John Maurath; Dr. Randy R. McGuire and the Saint Louis University Archives; the Missouri Civil War Museum; Missouri State Archives; National Archives and Bryan McGraw; Connie Nisinger; St. Louis Cardinals Media Relations and Christina Buck; Barbara and Mary Scott; Glenda Stockton; Virginia Todd; Mark Trout; University of Missouri-St. Louis, UMSL Library and Archives, Western Collections Managers; Jan Wilzbach; and Dr. John A. Wright.

Also, grateful thanks to our Arcadia family—Anna Wilson, John Pearson, and Elizabeth Bray—for their understanding and expertise.

INTRODUCTION

The vision, determination, and courage of the officers and soldiers of the numerous troops and divisions formed on and mustered through the complex demonstrate the reasons Jefferson Barracks remained an important installation from its inception in 1826 until it was declared surplus property in 1946. However, since the Missouri National Guard assumed ownership of the heart of the complex from the Army, it ensures that Jefferson Barracks remains the oldest operating military installation west of the Mississippi River.

The post served many functions over its active years, but there was a constant truth: Jefferson Barracks was a home of the citizen soldier—men and (eventually) women who stepped away from their regular lives when circumstances demanded. By stepping up to serve, they defended and secured the future of America for generations.

This book chronicles various episodes during the history of Jefferson Barracks and these soldiers. These are not the only stories there are to relate. The base housed many more officers and soldiers during its 12 active decades. The accounts to be told are endless, as is the courage of those who serve.

One

GO WEST!

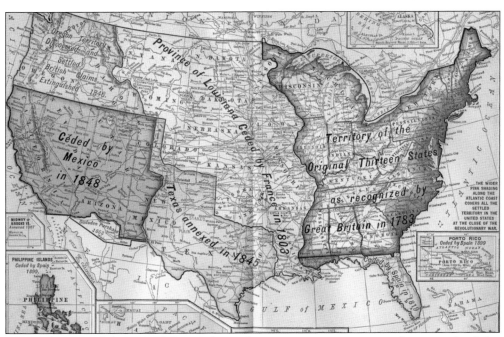

This early map of the United States shows the expansive segment gained as a result of the Louisiana Purchase of 1803. More than doubling the size of the country, the Louisiana Purchase rejuvenated the pioneer spirit and surged the population westward into previously unknown territories. The Mississippi River provided a natural boundary between the United States and its new area. Many Mississippi River towns, including St. Louis, saw growth in population, industry, and importance as a result of their locations. St. Louis's nickname, "the Gateway to the West," was a result of this happenstance. (Saint Louis University Archives, Dr. Randy McGuire; *St. Louis Arsenal: Armory of the West*.)

Meriwether Lewis (1774–1809) was one of the Corps of Discovery officers charged with mapping the newly purchased territory in 1803. He was a captain at the time. The expedition returned to Fort Bellefontaine on September 22, 1806, on its way to Washington, DC. In 1807, Lewis was appointed the second territorial governor. He died of gunshot wounds in 1809 at the age of 35. He had been en route to see President Jefferson, his childhood neighbor, who had selected him for the 1803 expedition. Whether he committed suicide or was murdered is still in question. (LOC, LC-USZ62-20214.)

William C. Clark (1770–1838) was the other half of the well-known exploratory team and was originally from Kentucky. After the famous three-year expedition, Clark became an Indian agent and brigadier general and was later the governor of the Territory of Missouri. He spent his retired life between St. Louis and his family home in Louisville, Kentucky. (LOC, LC-USZ62-10609.)

Early in the 19th century, Fort Bellefontaine, built on the banks of the Missouri River at Coldwater Creek above St. Louis, was the launching post for explorers like Zebulon Pike (1779–1813), pictured, and Henry Atkinson. They took troops west following Lewis and Clark's explorations. St. Louis was growing quickly. In 1770, its population was around 500. In 1806, the second year since its transfer from France, the population had grown to about 1,100. The city had 300 houses and several mercantile businesses. In 1808, the US government began a search for an area in which to build another fort to the north of Fort Bellefontaine. The post, relocated in 1811, consisted of 30 wooden buildings. (LOC, LC-USZ62-128057.)

By early 1826, Fort Bellefontaine was in an advanced state of disrepair. By order of the Commanding General of the Army, commanding general of the 6th Infantry Brevet Brig. Gen. Henry Atkinson (1782–1842); commander of the Western Department of the Army Brevet Maj. Gen. Edmund P. Gaines (1777–1849), who is pictured here; and Maj. Gen. Jacob J. Brown were ordered to find a suitable area to house a new concept for the Army—an infantry school of instruction. Gaines, Atkinson, William Clark, and Missouri governor John Miller searched together, starting at Fort Bellefontaine and proceeding south. Most of the land was too expensive for the government to buy. (Carondelet Historical Society.)

About 10 miles south of St. Louis City, the team found a village called Carondelet, named in honor of Francisco Luis Hector de Carondelet, the Spanish governor of the Louisiana Territory prior to its purchase by the United States. Founded in 1767, the small community—also referred to as Vide Poche (Empty Pocket)—had about 50 houses and nearly 250 residents in 1804. The illustration shows the village in 1826. (Dr. John A. Wright, *Carondelet*.)

The exploratory team of Gaines, Atkinson, Clark, and Miller agreed on a site in the south section of the 6,000 acres of Carondelet Commons. In 1826, a 1,702-acre tract of land was sold to the US government. The purchase document contained signatures of only 12 of Carondelet's landowners. The purchase price for the total acreage was a $5 gold coin. Descendants of early Carondelet residents have engaged in lawsuits to reverse the deed sale without success. This drawing shows Carondelet Road, which went through the village in 1826. Now called South Broadway, it still runs to Jefferson Barracks. (Saint Louis University Archives, Dr. Randy McGuire; *St. Louis Arsenal: Armory of the West*.)

The year 1826 was a pivotal time for the United States and its subsequent history. John Quincy Adams (1767–1848), pictured here, was president from 1825 to 1829. Both his father, the second president, John Adams (1735–1826); and the third president, Thomas Jefferson (1743–1826), died on July 4. (LOC, LC-USZ62-55283.)

A notice to the Army the following week announced the deaths of the two former presidents. The post was occupied on July 10, 1826, just a few days after the final purchase. On October 23, 1826, General Order No. 66 by the adjutant general declared the name of the new post as the Jefferson Barracks, after Thomas Jefferson (pictured). The barracks was also designated to be the first infantry school of practice (basic training facility) for the Army. (Saint Louis University Archives; Dr. Randy McGuire, St. Louis Arsenal: Armory of the West.)

Prior to that announcement, the new post was referred to both as Cantonment Adams, in honor of the sitting president, and as Cantonment Miller, named for John Miller (1781–1846), the fourth governor of Missouri from 1826 to 1832. Miller (pictured) also was an Army colonel in the War of 1812 and, after his stint as governor, served in the US House of Representatives. (Missouri State Archives.)

Upon selection of a site for the new fort, Stephen Watts Kearney, who was by then a brevet major, had been designated to bring the first troops to the new barracks. He arrived with four companies of the 1st Infantry on July 10, 1826, to found the post. Kearney's troops spent their early time at the new barracks constructing its buildings. (Marc Kollbaum.)

Although Kearney brought the first troops to the new installation, the title of commander was given to Gen. Henry Atkinson (1782–1842). Atkinson distinguished himself during the War of 1812. He led expeditions to the Yellowstone River in 1819 and 1825, establishing Fort Atkinson along the way. Atkinson was also well connected. Around the time he was placed in charge of the new barracks, he married Mary Bullitt of Louisville, Kentucky, who was a great-niece of William Clark of Lewis and Clark fame. Clark apparently introduced the couple. Early in January 1827, the newlyweds held the first military ball at the barracks. The building in which the ball was to be held was not finished. The dance was illuminated by candlelight. Soldiers placed candles on their rifles' bayonets and lined them around the perimeter of the room. William Clark, in attendance, reciprocated the next week with a ball held by the citizens of St. Louis to welcome the new military installation to the area. Atkinson remained the commander of Jefferson Barracks until his death in 1842. (Marc Kollbaum.)

Two

THE EARLY YEARS

This 1841 lithograph by John Caspar Wild is the earliest known depiction of Jefferson Barracks. It shows the original buildings surrounding the quadrangle. Troops are in formation in the upper center of the work. (Saint Louis University Archives, Dr. Randy McGuire, *St. Louis Arsenal: Armory of the West.*)

Henry Dodge (1782–1867) rose to military fame as a major general of the Missouri Militia in the War of 1812. He again served in the Black Hawk War of 1832, including the Battle of Bad Axe, as colonel of the western Michigan Territory militia. In 1832, he received a commission of Major of the Regiment of Mounted Rangers. The First Regiment of Dragoons replaced the troop the following year. Dodge served as colonel of the newly formed dragoons. This is believed to be an early photograph of Dodge. (LOC, LC-USZ62-109838.)

Another early resident of Jefferson Barracks was Benjamin Louis Eulalie de Bonneville (1796–1878), a French-born immigrant who was the godson of Thomas Paine, one of America's Founding Fathers. Bonneville graduated from the US Military Academy at West Point in 1815. Assigned in 1828 to Jefferson Barracks, Bonneville became intrigued with the ideas of exploration and completed many expeditions westward. Washington Irving wrote about Bonneville's exploits in a successful book. Bonneville also returned later to Jefferson Barracks to serve as a post commander in 1866. (Wikipedia.)

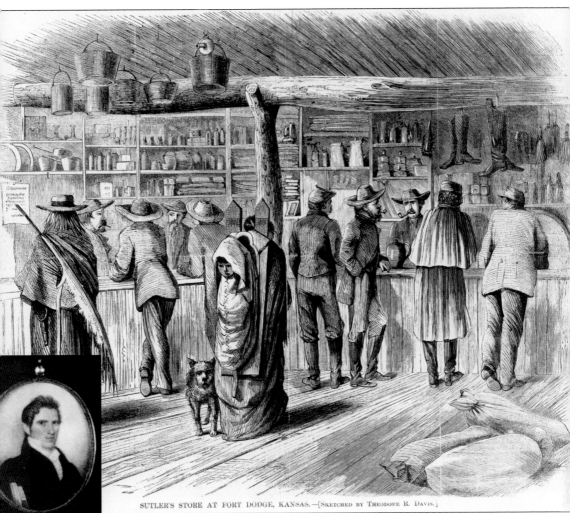

SUTLER'S STORE AT FORT DODGE, KANSAS. —[SKETCHED BY THEODORE R. DAVIS.]

George Hancock Kenerly (1790–1867), who is pictured in the inset, was born in Virginia. Attached to St. Louis during the War of 1812, he remained there, marrying Alize Menard, who was the daughter of Pierre Menard (1767–1844), the first lieutenant governor of Illinois. Kenerly and his brother James operated a successful mercantile business in St. Louis. George Kenerly also became the first postmaster for Jefferson Barracks and was its first sutler as well. His sister Harriet Kenerly married William Clark. A daughter from Harriet's first marriage married Stephen Watts Kearney. George's father, Samuel Kenerly, a Revolutionary War patriot, is believed to be buried somewhere on the grounds but not in the national cemetery. Pictured is the sutler's store at Fort Dodge, Kansas, during the same time period that Kenerly was running the sutler's store at Jefferson Barracks. (Inset, Kenerly Family History, Kedrick Kenerly; larger image, LOC, LC-USZ62-116768.)

MA-KA-TAI-ME-SHE-KIA-KIAH
BLACK HAWK A SAUKIE BRAVE
PUBLISHED BY F. W. GREENOUGH, PHILAD.ª

Ma-Ka-Tai-Me-She-Kia-Kiak (1767–1838), the chief of the Sauk and Fox aligned tribes, was better known as Black Hawk. Born in Saukenuk, near the confluence of the Mississippi and the Rock Rivers in northwestern Illinois, he was perhaps the son of Chief Pyesa. The 1804 Treaty of St. Louis gave all the Illinois and Iowa tribal lands near the Mississippi River to the white settlers. As whites began moving into those territories, tribes retaliated by siding with the British in the War of 1812. In 1828, Pres. John Quincy Adams ordered that the Sauk lands, at that time in Iowa, be sold. (Carondelet Historical Society.)

The tribes decided to fight to retain that land and to regain the land previously taken from them in Illinois as well. After speaking with William Clark in 1830, General Atkinson urged that no additional land be taken from the tribes. He sent troops to the area to spread the word and to supervise the removal of the whites from the land. War was avoided between the factions for two years. Black Hawk is pictured here in American attire. (LOC, LC-USZ62-86680.)

The Black Hawk War of 1832 was mounted largely from Jefferson Barracks, with most troops under the direct leadership of Gen. Henry Atkinson. Black Hawk was captured in August 1832 near the Wisconsin Dells with six of his most trusted men, and 2nd Lt. Jefferson Davis (1808–1889), pictured here, escorted them back to Jefferson Barracks. Black Hawk was taken east. He wanted to see the president, Andrew Jackson. During this trip, Black Hawk was briefly imprisoned at Fort Monroe, in Virginia. Ironically, this was the same prison in which Davis would be held following the Civil War. (Carondelet Historical Society.)

During their incarceration at Jefferson Barracks, Black Hawk and his men were kept in chains. The famous American writer Washington Irving (1783–1859), pictured, was brought to Jefferson Barracks to interview Black Hawk. The famous Western portrait artist George Catlin was also brought in to capture the famous warriors' images. All seven of the prisoners were taken to Washington, DC, in 1833 to meet Pres. Andrew Jackson. (LOC, LC-USZ62-103574.)

The Regiment of Dragoons was activated at Jefferson Barracks by an Act of Congress on March 2, 1833. Within the first year, Troops A–H were formed in Tennessee, New York, Kentucky, and Ohio, with three additional troops formed at Jefferson Barracks, which served as the headquarters. Dragoons were trained to fight both on horseback and on foot. They gained the designation of the First Regiment of Dragoons in 1836, when a second regiment was organized. (Marc Kollbaum.)

Some already familiar Jefferson Barracks names were associated with the early Dragoons. Col. Henry Dodge was the first commander, followed by Lt. Col. Stephen Watts Kearney when Dodge resigned in 1836 to assume an appointment as governor of Wisconsin. Henry Leavenworth (1783–1834), pictured here, commanded the First US Dragoons in 1834. He died in July 1834, perhaps from a wound incurred during a buffalo hunt. (Carondelet Historical Society.)

Nathan Boone (1781–1856), pictured in the inset, was the tenth and last child of Daniel (in the larger image) and Rebecca Bryan Boone. He joined the Dragoons near their formation and rose to captain. Another original captain was Edwin Voss Sumner (1797–1863), who became commander of Jefferson Barracks in 1850. Jefferson Davis was a first lieutenant in the new Dragoons, transferring from the 1st Infantry. James Clyman (1792–1881), one of the regiment's original second lieutenants, encountered the Donner Party on his return from the far west and urged them to turn back—advice they did not take. Richard Barnes Mason (1797–1850), an early lieutenant, followed Kearney as military governor of California in 1847. He died at Jefferson Barracks in 1850. (Both, Marc Kollbaum.)

DRED SCOTT.

In the 1830s, Dr. John Emerson moved west to St. Louis, where he reported for duty at Jefferson Barracks. He had traveled to St. Louis with the family of Capt. Peter Blow, who sold him one of their slaves, a man named Dred Scott. Scott (1799–1858) married a young slave named Harriet Robinson. (LOC, LC-USZ62-5092.)

Robert E. Lee (1807–1870) was second in his 1829 class at West Point and was a new brevet second lieutenant with the Army Corps of Engineers when he was sent to Jefferson Barracks for engineering work. One of his tasks was to improve the condition of the riverbanks along the Mississippi River and their impact on St. Louis and the area. The ports were being destroyed by sand and silt. Lee's solutions involved measures that eventually also submerged the infamous Bloody Island—the scene of many duels involving locals. He solved both problems. (Marc Kollbaum.)

This sundial is one of the oldest artifacts of Jefferson Barracks. It has not moved since it arrived in 1841 but now stands in front of the Administration Building, which was built in 1900. The picture was taken in the 1890s. (Marc Kollbaum.)

Ulysses S. Grant (1822–1885) graduated from West Point in 1843. His first assignment as a young second lieutenant was at Jefferson Barracks. The Mexican-American War was declared by Congress on May 13, 1846. Grant commanded troops mounted at Jefferson Barracks, which served as a staging post for the war. A regiment of 11 companies sent to New Orleans became known as the St. Louis Legion. (LOC, LC-USZ62-110718.)

During the war, Grant learned war strategies and logistics from two generals whom he greatly admired. The first was Zachary Taylor (1784–1850), pictured here. He was known as "Old Rough and Ready." His military career included the War of 1812, the Second Seminole War, and the Black Hawk War, in which he accepted the surrender of Chief Black Hawk. Taylor's actions in the battles of the Mexican-American War impressed more than the young Grant. His endeavors won him the acclaim of the American people as well as the 1848 presidential election. He died in his second year of office. (Carondelet Historical Society.)

25

WINFIELD SCOTT.
MAJOR GEN.ᵗ OF THE U.S ARMY.

Winfield Scott (1786–1866) was the other general Grant studied. Scott served his country from the War of 1812 forward. Winning many decisive battles, including the Battle of Churubusco (pictured below), Scott was a national hero following the Mexican-American War. The Mexican forces sustained nearly twice the casualties as the Americans. Winning this battle on August 20, 1847, placed the US military within five miles of Mexico City. A month later, Mexican troops were defeated in Mexico City, ending the war. (Left, Carondelet Historical Society; below, LOC, LC-USZ62-48765.)

BATTLE OF CHURUBUSCO, NEAR THE CITY OF MEXICO.
AUG. 19ᵀᴴ & 20ᵀᴴ 1847.

CO! HARNEY AT THE DRAGOON FIGHT AT MEDELIN, NEAR VERA CRUZ.
MARCH 25th 1847.

Benjamin Harney, an Army surgeon, asked Andrew Jackson for a letter of recommendation to get his brother William Selby Harney (1800–1889), pictured in this lithograph, into the Navy. William Harney served during the Seminole Wars and the Black Hawk War with the 1st US Infantry. Joining Winfield Scott's troops as an officer, Harney took command of the Second Dragoons from Jefferson Barracks as a colonel in the Mexican-American War. As such, he was the hero of several battles, including the one depicted here in Currier and Ives' *Col. Harney at the Dragoon fight at Medelin, near Vera Cruz: March 25, 1847.* (LOC, LC-USZ62-2119.)

The nameless citizen soldiers were the heart of the war, fighting the battles on a daily basis. The stories of these citizen soldiers, as well as their names, are often lost in history. This young man was a member of the Missouri Volunteers in the Mexican-American War. (Marc Kollbaum.)

In 1848, with the short and successful Mexican-American War completed, Jefferson Barracks returned to its relatively normal daily routines. It experienced tremendous growth in the early 1850s. The abundant limestone in the Mississippi River Valley created many limestone quarries along the riverbanks. A quarry was also on the Jefferson Barracks campus, providing the limestone for new structures built on the barracks in that decade. This massive wall was constructed around much of the facility, including the cemetery, in 1851. (Carondelet Historical Society.)

This is a side view of the Ordnance Magazine, built of limestone in the early to mid-1850s. Ordnance and powder magazines both stored gunpowder, cannonballs, and other ammunition used by the troops. The doors are in the middle. This view shows the iron gate and part of the wall surrounding the building. The roof was built to blow skyward in the event of destruction, so that the contents and the structure would not blow outward, which would cause greater damage. (Marc Kollbaum.)

The Laborers' House (right) was part of the limestone construction boom during this decade. The building housed various nonmilitary laborers who were brought in for construction work. This photograph also shows the stable (center), which still stands, and the kitchen (left), which no longer exists. (Marc Kollbaum.)

No stone was left unturned, so to speak, in using the plentiful limestone. Even the new enlisted men's barracks were constructed of limestone in the 1850s. (Carondelet Historical Society.)

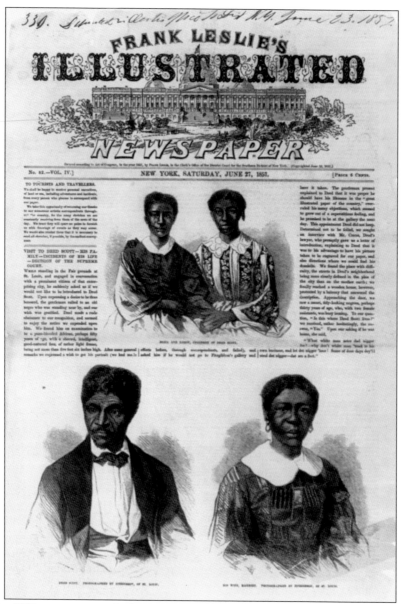

While the 1850s were times of relative peace, there was a strong undercurrent of impending turmoil brewing in the United States. Much of the construction at Jefferson Barracks during this decade was in preparation for whatever was to come next. Earlier in the decade, the St. Louis and Iron Mountain Railroad had petitioned Congress for the right-of-way through the barracks. The Iron Mountain Railroad's president was Henry Blow, son of the original owner of Dred Scott. The Army opposed the proposed right-of-way, stating that tracks were too close to the ordnance magazines on the northeast side of the base. The Army counterproposed the trains' steam engines be shut down and all trains pulled by mules through the section fronting the barracks. The request by the railroad was granted in 1853 without the Army's additional suggestion. The Dred Scott cases lasted much of the decade. Scott had been owned by Emerson, a doctor in the US Army, who had taken Scott with him. His assignments included Jefferson Barracks in Missouri, a slave state, and Fort Armstrong in Illinois, a free state. (Dr. John A. Wright.)

Three

THE WAR BETWEEN THE STATES AND WITHIN MISSOURI

By the time the Civil War erupted on April 12, 1861, at Fort Sumter, South Carolina, William Selby Harney, a hero of the Mexican-American War, was commander of Jefferson Barracks. Promoted to full brigadier general in 1858, Harney was named post commander in 1860. When the Civil War broke out, Harney was one of only four regular generals in the US Army. Missouri was designated an armed-neutral state during the administration of Gov. Robert Marcellus Stewart (1815–1871), who was the 14th governor of Missouri from 1857 to 1861. As such, Missouri, while remaining part of the United States, was to not send men or money to either the Union or the Confederate side. Harney's family home in Sullivan, Missouri, still stands. (LOC, LC-DIG-cwpb-04404.)

In March 1861, Nathaniel Lyon (1818–1861), who had served in the Seminole Wars and the Mexican-American War, arrived in St. Louis as the commander of Company D of the 2nd Infantry. Concerned about possible Missouri secession, Lyon asked prominent St. Louisan and fellow veteran Francis P. Blair Jr. to help him to be named commander of the Arsenal Building in St. Louis in May 1861. (Carondelet Historical Society.)

The St. Louis Arsenal, under the management of Nathaniel Lyon, is pictured here as seen from the west. The walls of the main building were constructed of limestone from local quarries. (Saint Louis University Archives, Dr. Randy McGuire; *St. Louis Arsenal: Armory of the West.*)

After receiving a letter from President Lincoln requesting troops, Gov. Claiborne Fox Jackson ordered Missouri State Guard troops to meet at the Missouri State Militia Camp at Liddell's Grove, which is now part of the campus of Saint Louis University, to train for home defense. Upon hearing this, Nathaniel Lyon, pictured, supposedly went to the location dressed as an old woman to do surveillance, subsequently claiming that Governor Jackson had plans to seize the arsenal and its contents for the purpose of arming troops to fight against the Union. (LOC, LC-USZ62-75140.)

MAJOR LYON.

THE FIRST CLASH WEST OF THE MISSISSIPPI   CAMP JACKSON, ST. LOUIS, MISSOURI, MAY, 1861

The following day, May 10, 1861, Lyon and his regiment went to Camp Jackson in St. Louis and captured those troops who had mustered, as commanded by Governor Jackson. Lyon marched the prisoners along the streets of St. Louis. Riots ensued as those sympathetic to the Southern cause rebelled against seeing fellow citizens paraded through town. Lyon's troops responded by opening fire, although the source of the first shots is still questioned, and 28 civilians were killed and more than 75 wounded. Also killed in the Camp Jackson Affair were three militia and two federal soldiers, including Captain Blandowski, making him the first officer killed in battle in the Civil War. Blandowski has a memorial stone at Jefferson Barracks National Cemetery. (LOC, LC-USZ62-132566.)

Missouri's determination to remain neutral was challenged early in May, 1861. There was already unrest between various factions in the state. Governor Claiborne Fox Jackson, pictured, was pro-Confederate, and, from the time he took office January 2, 1861, worked to see Missouri secede from the Union. The new governor was thwarted earlier in the year by a better than three-to-one vote at the Missouri state convention to side with the Union. He decided to retain the "armed neutral" designation of his predecessor. President Lincoln sent Jackson a letter ordering the Missouri governor to supply four state regiments to the Union to fight against the South. Jackson refused. Secretly, Jackson was sending money and goods to the Confederates and continuing to work clandestinely toward secession. (Saint Louis University Archives, Dr. Randy McGuire, *St. Louis Arsenal: Armory of the West*.)

From the neighbourhood of Boonville, Mo. on the 18th inst a mischievous JACK who was frightened and run away from his Leader by the sudden appearance of a Lion. He is of no value whatever and only a low PRICE can be given for his capture. *Sam*.

By June 1861, Nathaniel Lyon and his troops had driven Governor Jackson from Jefferson City, the Missouri state capital. Lyon caught up with Jackson and Sterling Price, who was now a general for the Confederacy, in Boonville, Missouri, on June 17. Jackson and Price had a unit of men traveling to join the Confederates. Lyon's men won the conflict. This political cartoon portrays Lyon as his animal namesake and Jackson as an ass. The cartoon, in the manner of a "lost animal" sign of the times, says the ass is "of no value whatever and only a low Price can be given for his capture." (LOC, LC-USZ62-14953.)

Sterling Price (1809–1867) was a state representative of Missouri from 1836 to 1838 and 1840 to 1844, and then served in the 29th US Congress from 1845 until he resigned in 1846 to participate in the Mexican-American War. Returning home to Missouri a hero, Price was named a brigadier general in 1847. He was elected the 13th governor of Missouri from 1853 to 1857. Originally, he opposed Missouri's secession from the Union, but Price was so outraged by the actions of the Camp Jackson Affair that he became a Southern sympathizer. Governor Jackson placed him in command of the Missouri State Guard, newly reconfigured by Jackson to support the Confederate cause. (LOC, LC-DIG-cwpb-07527.)

The situation soon came to a violent head. By mid-July, Lyon was in Springfield, Missouri, with about 6,000 Union troops. General Price was south of him, waiting to meet with other Confederate leaders near the Missouri southern border. The combined Confederate troops, mostly Missouri State Guard members, numbered near 12,000 as they marched north together to seize Springfield and remove Lyon and his Union troops. On August 10, 1861, the two factions met in the six-hour Battle of Wilson's Creek, also known as the Battle of Oak Hills, near Springfield. General Lyon was mortally wounded, leading a final charge. This was the first major battle of the Civil War west of the Mississippi. (LOC, LC-USZ62-121404.)

Francis Preston Blair Jr. (1821–1875) was a politician and lawyer. He was a member of the House of Representatives from Missouri for several terms and was nominated by the Democratic Party as the 1868 vice presidential candidate. He served as senator from Missouri from 1871 to 1873. A friend of Nathaniel Lyon, Blair helped Lyon become commander of the St. Louis Arsenal and assisted him in the actions of the Camp Jackson Affair. (Saint Louis University Archives, Dr. Randy McGuire; *St. Louis Arsenal: Armory of the West.*)

Blair rose from the rank of colonel in the 1st Regiment of Missouri Volunteers. He was promoted to brigadier general of volunteers in August 1862 and then to major general in November 1862. He is pictured here with his staff during the Civil War. From left to right are (first row) Brevet Brig. Gen. A. Hickenlooper, Maj. Gen. Francis Blair, and Maj. Charles Cadle; (second row) Capt. G.R. Steele, Capt. William Henley (29th Missouri Infantry), Maj. Phil Tompkins, and Lt. Col. D.T. Kirby (29th Missouri Infantry). (LOC, LC- USZ62-15344.)

This lithograph describes Jefferson Barracks in St. Louis, Missouri, as "lately the scene of great excitement on the departure of the Fourth Regiment of Missouri Volunteers to take possession of Bird's Point, Missouri, opposite Cairo, Illinois. Busy scene." Also known as the Battle of Charleston, the Union forces led by Col. Henry Dougherty successfully destroyed a Confederate camp. The lithograph originally was in Frank Leslie's illustrated newspaper on June 29, 1861. (LOC, LC-USZ61-1867.)

William Tecumseh Sherman (1820–1891) was from Ohio, but he considered St. Louis his home. A graduate of West Point in 1840, he served in the Seminole Wars and then was sent to California in an administrative role. He accompanied military governor Col. Richard Barnes Mason on the inspection to verify the discovery of gold that led to the California Gold Rush. Sherman was attached to Jefferson Barracks in 1850, but he resigned from the military and became a businessman in St. Louis by 1853. (LOC, LC-USZ62-72803.)

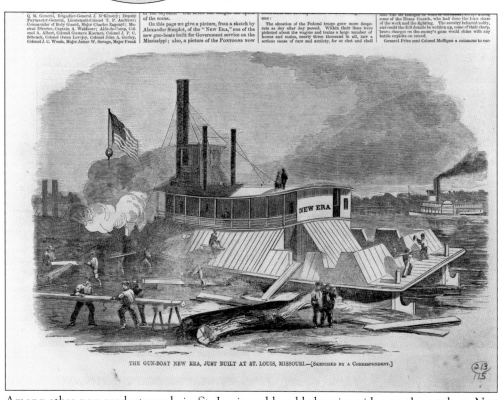

The War between the States, a term coined in the South that remained prevalent in that region after the Civil War, lasted from 1861 to 1865 and was recognized as the first industrialized war. From knives to uniforms to boats, items of war became items of duplication. St. Louis was in the forefront of industrialization. James Buchanan Eads (1820–1887), an engineer and inventor, was contracted in August 1861 to construct seven identical ironclad ships by October 5, 1861. Extensive penalties would be levied if Eads did not have the ships ready on time, which he did not. His ironclad ships were all named after cities. (LOC, LC-USZ62-62148.)

THE GUN-BOAT NEW ERA, JUST BUILT AT ST. LOUIS, MISSOURI.—[SKETCHED BY A CORRESPONDENT.]

Among other new products made in St. Louis and heralded nationwide was the gunboat *New Era*, which was built in 1861. (LOC, LC-USZ62-108449.)

Not all soldiers in the Civil War were natural-born Americans. During the 1840s and 1850s, Missouri enjoyed an increase in immigrants from Germany and surrounding areas. Many settled in the St. Louis area. One of these immigrants was Gustav Heinrichs. Born on May 18, 1828, in Germany, he made his living as an author and journalist. He fought for his new, adopted home during the Civil War, rising through the ranks from first lieutenant in the 3rd Missouri Infantry, to major in the 4th and 5th Missouri Cavalry, and finally to lieutenant colonel in the 41st Missouri Infantry. He died in St. Louis on January 20, 1874, and was buried in Jefferson Barracks National Cemetery, Section OPS1, grave no. 2210. (Carondelet Historical Society.)

Ulysses S. Grant returned to Jefferson Barracks several times during the summer of 1861. In 1848, Grant had married Julia Boggs Dent (1826–1902), from St. Louis. He resigned his commission around 1854 and struggled for several years to make a living. Finally, he and his young family returned to Grant's childhood home in Galena, Illinois, where he clerked in his family's tannery business. He reenlisted shortly after the war broke out, first serving as a training officer near Cairo, Illinois. (Marc Kollbaum.)

Julia Boggs Dent was the daughter of "Colonel" Frederick Dent and Ellen Bray Wrenshall Dent. She was born and raised on White Haven, a successful southern estate in Affton, a suburb of St. Louis. Her older brother Frederick was Ulysses Grant's roommate at West Point. Julia first met Grant in 1844 when he came home with Frederick for vacation. The couple kept their engagement secret for over a year, fearing her father would disapprove since Grant earned only a soldier's pay. They married at White Haven on August 22, 1848, after Grant's return from the Mexican-American War. (LOC, LC-USZ62-101867.)

The saying that politics and wars make strange bedfellows was true during the Civil War—brother fought brother and neighbor fought neighbor. The Grant family was no less impacted. Grant's family, who lived in Ohio and Illinois, were staunch abolitionists. Julia Dent's family owned slaves. The groom's family was so appalled with that fact that they boycotted Ulysses' 1848 wedding. Pictured in this family portrait, dated between 1865 and 1873, from left to right are Julia Dent Grant; daughter Ellen "Nellie" Wrenshall Grant (1855–1922); Julia's father, "Colonel" Frederick Dent (1786–1873); and son Jesse Root Grant (1858–1934). (LOC, LC-DIG-cwpbh-004778.)

James Longstreet was a member of the West Point class of 1842. He and Ulysses S. Grant became friends while at West Point. Longstreet spent the first two post-graduation years at Jefferson Barracks, so he and Grant served there together for a while. Longstreet, who was Julia's fourth cousin, served as best man at Grant's wedding. Grant and his friend were on opposite sides of the Civil War as Longstreet became one of the most prominent Confederate generals. (Marc Kollbaum.)

Less than a year after the war's onset, ironclads, including the Carondelet (pictured) and others built by Eads, were engaged in lengthy combat from February 28 through April 8, 1862. In the Siege of Island Number 10, Union forces were triumphant over this Confederate stronghold on the Mississippi River. (LOC, LC-USZ62-67468.)

In 1862, Samuel Langhorne Clemens, better known as Mark Twain, served a two-week stint in the Confederate Army, quitting after being frustrated by numerous retreats. He had joined the troops that General Grant ran out of Clemens's Hannibal, Missouri, area. During his short service, Clemens was on a steamboat that unsuccessfully tried to run the blockade at Jefferson Barracks. Two holes were shot through the steamboat's smokestacks. (LOC, LC-USZ62-28851.)

In 1862, Jefferson Barracks became one of the nation's largest medical centers. Union wounded were treated at the Jefferson Barracks General Hospital, pictured here as it looked during the Civil War. (Marc Kollbaum.)

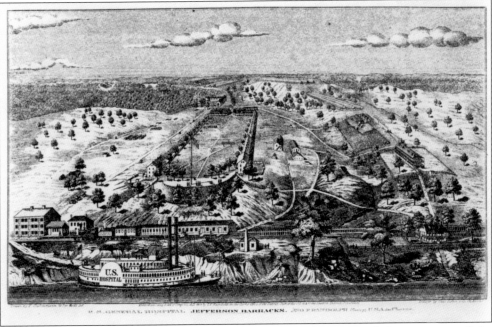

Jefferson Barracks added three temporary hospitals, seen here around the perimeter of the installation, during the war. Dr. John Field Randolph, in charge of the Department of the Missouri, became the major surgeon, serving in that capacity until the end of the Civil War. This lithograph was mass-produced in 1864 and given away at the St. Louis conference of the Western Sanitary Commission in 1864. (Carondelet Historical Society.)

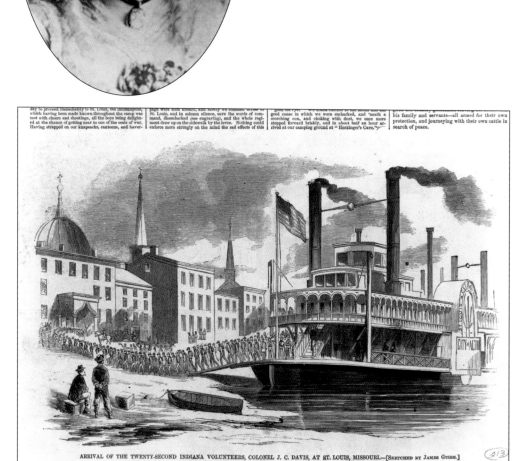

The US Sanitary Commission started in 1861 to aid the Army Medical Bureau. Following the Wilson's Creek battle, it was apparent that available care for the wounded in the West was lacking, so the Western Sanitary Commission was headquartered in St. Louis on September 5, 1861. A major faction of this commission became the St. Louis Ladies Union Aid Society, a group of society ladies in the area. They donated time, materials, and supplies to the wounded in the various area hospitals. One of the group's leaders, Jessie Benton Fremont (1824–1902), was the daughter of Missouri senator Thomas Hart Benton and the wife of John C. Fremont. She was an author and political activist. (Wikimedia Commons.)

ARRIVAL OF THE TWENTY-SECOND INDIANA VOLUNTEERS, COLONEL J. C. DAVIS, AT ST. LOUIS, MISSOURI.—[SKETCHED BY JAMES GUIRE.]

By late March 1862, the Western Sanitation Commission converted numerous steamships into floating hospitals. Transport boats, like this one, the *City of Alton*, were used for moving the injured and sick to both floating and land hospitals. This illustration is the *Arrival of the Twenty-Second Indiana Volunteers in St. Louis* (1861), under the direction of Colonel J.C. Davis. (LOC, LC-USZ62-12965.)

John Charles Fremont (1813–1890), a colorful figure, was an explorer, military figure, military governor of California, a senator from California, and the first presidential candidate of the Republican Party (1856). He was often the center of controversy, like the one that arose after he replaced Harney as commander of the Army's Department of the West, headquartered at Jefferson Barracks, in 1861. Following the Wilson's Creek fiasco and Lyon's death, Fremont placed Missouri under martial law. President Lincoln asked Fremont to rescind the order, but Fremont refused. Lincoln publicly revoked the martial law and relieved Fremont of command. In 1862, Fremont was placed in charge of the Army's Mountain Department of Tennessee, Kentucky, and Virginia. (LOC, LC-USZ62-107503.)

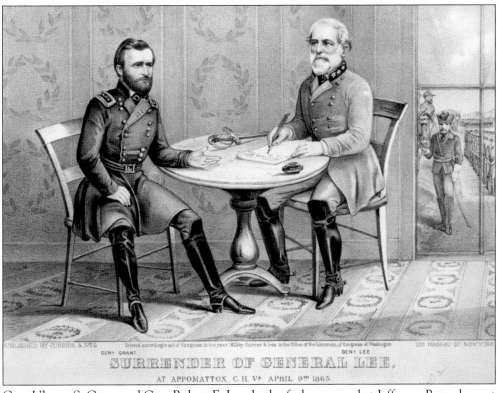

Gen. Ulysses S. Grant and Gen. Robert E. Lee, both of whom served at Jefferson Barracks, met as the opposing Union and Confederate generals at Appomattox Court House, Virginia, on April 9, 1865. There, Lee signed papers surrendering to Grant, ending, on paper, the Civil War. (LOC, LC-USZ62-3054.)

Most major players of the Civil War, on both sides, were stationed at Jefferson Barracks at some time during their military careers. Among those on the Union side was Don Carlos Buell (1818–1898). An 1841 West Point graduate, Buell was stationed at Jefferson Barracks as a second lieutenant in the 3rd Infantry. He served in the Seminole War and the Mexican-American War. In the Civil War, he was a major general and led Union troops in the Battle of Shiloh and the Battle of Perryville. (Marc Kollbaum.)

Winfield Scott Hancock (1824-1886), an 1844 West Point graduate, was in the Mexican-American War. Following that, while an officer at Jefferson Barracks, he met and married a St. Louis woman. Hancock was often cited for his leadership in the Civil War, especially as major general at the Battle of Gettysburg in 1863. He was the 1880 Democratic Party's nominee for president. (Marc Kollbaum.)

Among the generals for the Confederate States of America (CSA) was Braxton Bragg (1817–1876). An 1837 West Point graduate, Bragg served in the Second Seminole War. He was stationed at Jefferson Barracks during the Mexican-American War and placed in charge of reorganizing Batteries B and C of the 3rd Artillery. These troops eventually joined Zachary Taylor's forces. Bragg was promoted twice in 1861, first to brigadier general by March and then to major general by September. (Marc Kollbaum.)

Another prominent Confederate general was Joseph E. Johnston (1807–1891). An 1829 West Point graduate, he was a classmate of Robert E. Lee. A career officer who served in the Seminole Wars and the Mexican-American War, Johnston became commander of Jefferson Barracks in 1856. Named the Quartermaster General of the US Army in June 1860, he resigned in April 1861 to join the Confederate army. Leaving the Union army as a brigadier general, he was the highest-ranking Union officer who resigned to join the Confederacy. He rose through Confederate ranks to full general. Learning of Lee's surrender to Grant, Johnston surrendered to Gen. William Tecumseh Sherman on April 26, 1865. His death in 1891 was supposedly caused by a cold he caught while marching in General Sherman's funeral procession through the streets of St. Louis. (Marc Kollbaum.)

This lithograph, titled *Abraham Lincoln's Last Reception*, may depict an event on one of those days after Appomattox and before April 14, 1865. It shows the Lincolns greeting and mingling with cabinet members, Union generals Grant and Sherman, and Lincoln's successor, then vice president Andrew Johnson. (LOC, LC-USZ62-12824.)

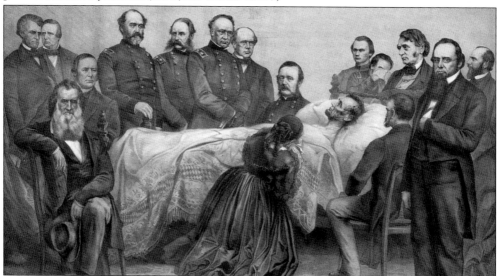

Within days of the Confederate surrender to the Union, the United States was dealt a blow—the assassination of Pres. Abraham Lincoln on April 14, 1865. In addition to his wife, Mary Todd Lincoln, Lincoln's deathbed was surrounded by Edwin Stanton, secretary of war; Dr. Joseph K. Barnes, surgeon general of the US Army; Dr. Charles Henry Crane, surgeon general of the United States; Dr. Charles Leale, a young Army surgeon who happened to be attending the play at Ford's Theater that fateful night; and, among others, Henry Wager Halleck, named general-in-chief of all the armies by Lincoln in 1862. (LOC, LC-USZ62-7443.)

Henry Wager Halleck played a large role in the history of Jefferson Barracks. As commander of the Department of the Missouri, Halleck informed secretary of war Edwin Stanton on March 28, 1862, that he had ordered the evacuation of Jefferson Barracks, turning the buildings over to the Medical Department for use as a hospital facility. (LOC, LC-DIG-cwpb-04718.)

Early in its history, Jefferson Barracks established the Post Cemetery. The first interment at the cemetery was Eliza Ann Lash, the young daughter of an officer stationed there. In April 1862, a War Department order told the various department commanders to provide for appropriate burials for those fallen in Civil War battles. (Sandie Grassino.)

Halleck, commanding general of the Department of the West, completed the process to turn the Jefferson Barracks Post Cemetery into a national cemetery. An 1866 Congressional order established the change. In 1868, a report to the secretary of war stated that 8,601 burials had taken place to date at Jefferson Barracks National Cemetery. This is an 1890s photograph of the entrance to the national cemetery. (Carondelet Historical Society.)

This hand-tinted 19th-century postcard is an early view of the cemetery. The cannon in the illustration is one of several in this section of the cemetery. (Carondelet Historical Society.)

Four

RECONSTRUCTION, CONSTRUCTION, AND WARS

The Reconstruction era was pivotal in America's history. Repairing the damages of the Civil War proved lengthy. It took four years for all seceded states to be readmitted to the union and receive Congressional representation. Jefferson Barracks, no longer needed as a major medical facility, again pursued its title of Gateway to the West. This illustration, originally in *Harper's Weekly* (vol. 11, no. 536) is dated April 6, 1867, which was nearly two years to the day from the end of the Civil War. Its title, *the New Commanders in the Surrectionary States*, shows the powerful men leading America forward. Many of them had major roles at Jefferson Barracks. Pictured on horseback, from left to right, are Daniel Edgar Sickles, John Pope, George Henry Thomas, Ulysses S. Grant, John McAllister Schofield, Philip Henry Sheridan, and Edward Otho Cresap Ord. (LOC, LC-USZ62-127611.)

On July 24, 1866, the US government approved the creation of new infantry and cavalry units at Jefferson Barracks. The units were comprised of freed slaves and other blacks, many of whom had served in the Civil War. These troops, both infantry and cavalry, were sent west to fight in the numerous Indian wars of the period. The men became known as the Buffalo Soldiers because the Indians thought the soldiers' hair resembled that of the buffalo. Shown in the picture are the typical uniform and equipment for a member of the 9th and 10th Cavalries, formed at Jefferson Barracks. Undoubtedly, the most famous buffalo soldier was the only woman known to serve in its ranks. Cathay Williams (1842–after 1892) was born a slave and worked as a housemaid for a wealthy planter from Jefferson City, Missouri. Freed by Union soldiers, she became a paid servant for the Union Army. Philip Sheridan took her to Washington, DC, as his cook. She traveled with the troops to several battles. After the war, she joined the newly formed Company A in St. Louis disguised as a man, William Cathay. Apparently, the entrance physical examination for the regiment was lax because she was approved. She was stationed at Jefferson Barracks from February to June 1867 when her company marched to Kansas and eventually to New Mexico. She served until 1868. (Jefferson Barracks Heritage Foundation Museum, Bill Florich.)

While the Buffalo Soldiers troops were African American, their commanders were traditionally white, including their first general, Benjamin Henry Grierson (1826–1911). A music teacher by profession, Grierson became a Union general with the cavalry during the Civil War. He created the diversionary "Grierson's Raid" as part of General Grant's campaign into Vicksburg in 1863, marching over 800 miles. Grierson organized the 10th Cavalry in 1866, insisting it be referred to as the US 10th Cavalry rather than as the 10th Colored Cavalry. He drew criticism from some officers, including Gen. Philip Sheridan, who questioned his trust and faith in his troops. Grierson attained the rank of brigadier general in April 1890 and retired in July of that year. (Marc Kollbaum.)

William Babcock Hazen (1830–1887), who graduated West Point in 1855, was a childhood friend of future president James A. Garfield. He was named commander of the 38th Infantry and made post commander of Jefferson Barracks, taking charge January 30, 1867. By the time of his arrival, nearly 250 soldiers were in the 38th Infantry at Jefferson Barracks. (LOC, LC-USZ62-104939.)

Peter Conover Hains (1840–1921), an 1861 West Point graduate, finished the academy with George Armstrong Custer (1839–1876). Hains ranked no. 19 in the class, and Custer was no. 34, last in the class. Hains, a Union officer in the Civil War, was named commander of Jefferson Barracks in October 1867. During his three commanding years at the post, he drilled troops in techniques of trench-digging and bridge construction as well as in infantry procedures. Relieved of his command in November 1870, he later served in the Spanish-American War and World War I, achieving the rank of major general. (LOC, LC-B811-4348.)

During Reconstruction, Jefferson Barracks realized a utilization dilemma. Its supportive function as a military hospital facility during the Civil War was no longer needed. The temporary hospitals were torn down. By 1871, Jefferson Barracks realized a new purpose as an ordnance site. The St. Louis Arsenal closed, and its contents were removed to Jefferson Barracks. Carlisle Barracks, opened by George Washington during the American Revolution, also closed, and its contents also were moved to Jefferson Barracks. President Grant and other dignitaries made a rail visit to the barracks on the Iron Mountain Railroad, in a special train car furnished by the railroad president. They stopped at the barracks depot pictured here. (Carondelet Historical Society.)

Jefferson Barracks was again poised to deploy troops to protect the West through expeditions and peacekeeping missions. The emphases were now on the Southwest and Northwest. This drawing from the June 18, 1870, edition of *Harper's Weekly*, titled *Let Us Have Peace*, shows President Grant extending his hand to members of a delegation visiting Ely Parker, the commissioner of Indian Affairs. Peace was not to be, however. The decade showed increased hostility between Americans and the Apaches in the Southwest and the Lakota, as well with other tribes, in the Great Plains. (LOC, LC-USZ62-96533.)

Eugene Asa Carr (1830–1910), an 1850 West Point graduate, came to Jefferson Barracks in 1851, where he stayed until 1852. A veteran of the Battle of Wilson's Creek, he was also at the Battle of Vicksburg. He returned to Jefferson Barracks in the 1870s as post commander and was a leading force in several of the Indian Wars, including the Battle of Fort Apache (site seen below). Carr was a Medal of Honor recipient in 1894 for his Civil War performance as a general. (Left, LOC, LC-USZ62-90943; below, LOC, LC-dig-ppmsca-10049.)

The First Dragoons became the 1st Regiment of Cavalry on August 3, 1861, and Jefferson Barracks was named the Cavalry Depot in 1878. Their uniform was glorified and romanticized in the mid-20th century in a myriad of westerns. The cavalry's signature hat, known as the Hardee hat, was named after William Joseph Hardee, an early cavalry leader. The hat was worn by the Army beginning with the Civil War. For this multiunit hat, the designated colors were scarlet for artillery, blue for infantry, and yellow for cavalry. Hats in the cavalry and artillery were pinned up on the right, while those in the infantry were pinned up on the left. (Photograph in public domain per copyright holder, Gettysburg National Military Park Museum.)

William Joseph Hardee (1815–1873), an 1838 West Point graduate, became a second lieutenant in the Second Dragoons at Jefferson Barracks. He served under Zachary Taylor and Winfield Scott in the Mexican-American War. Hardee wrote the Army manual *Cavalry Tactics* and taught the subject at West Point in the late 1850s. Hardee served as a lieutenant general in the Confederacy, surrendering with Joseph E. Johnston to General Sherman at Durham Station, North Carolina. (LOC, LC-USZ62-14973.)

In the next decade, numerous expeditions explored the West. In late 1882, Gen. Philip Sheridan, who had been stationed at Jefferson Barracks as a captain at the beginning of the Civil War, urged the war department against the Yellowstone Park Improvement Company leasing parklands to private companies. The company also planned to put a railroad through the park. The toll taken on wildlife and minerals in the areas would be devastating, according to Sheridan, whose love of the park was noted in 1871, when Mount Sheridan was named for him. Conservationists and environmentalists alike widely encouraged Sheridan's pleas. In early 1883, Pres. Chester Arthur (1829–1886) and his presidential party visited Yellowstone National Park. In the group, from left to right, are John Schuyler Crosby (1839–1913), then governor of Montana; Lt. Col. Michael V. Sheridan; Lt. Gen. Philip Sheridan; Anson Stager (1825–1885), brevet brigadier general during the Civil War and president of Western Union Electrical Company; unidentified; Pres. Chester A. Arthur; unidentified; unidentified; Robert Todd Lincoln (1843–1926), son of Pres. Abraham Lincoln and 35th secretary of war under presidents Garfield and Arthur; and George G. Vest (1830–1904), a senator from Missouri, who pushed Congress for adoption of Sheridan's plea. Sheridan was appointed the commanding general of the Army on November 1, 1883, the same day that William Tecumseh Sherman resigned the post. (LOC, LC-USZ62-137259.)

Barracks troops engaged in many activities while waiting for deployment, including team sports. The team pictured here, thought to be one of the first at the installation, is the Jefferson Barracks baseball club. This photograph, from the late 1880s, is believed to be the last of two of the players, 7th Cavalry members who were killed at the Action at Wounded Knee Creek in South Dakota, on December 29, 1890. From left to right are (first row) Smith, third base; York, shortstop; Lewis, catcher; Teary, second base; and Gallagher, left field; (second row) Lindsey, right field; Getty, center field; Thomason, manager, captain, and shortstop; Clinton, pitcher; and Haigh, first base. Only the players' surnames are known. (Mark Trout.)

The railroad was widely used during this time period for troops. However, horse, mules, and stables were prominent at Jefferson Barracks. (Marc Kollbaum.)

The cavalry needed to provide for its animals both on the base and on the road. In addition to medical doctors, Jefferson Barracks also had veterinarians on the base. They would often accompany the cavalry on missions. (Marc Kollbaum.)

This photograph captures the cavalry preparing to deploy from Jefferson Barracks on a mission. Along with the men and horses, the entourage also would include a mule train carrying supplies and provisions for the long trek. At times, there were as many as 1,500 mules and 1,200 horses attached to the barracks. (Carondelet Historical Society.)

Cuba tried to break free from Spain for decades. America watched the attempts with interest. Finally, Cuba gained independence on January 1, 1898. Eleven days later, however, riots erupted in Havana. The USS *Maine*, sent to Havana by Pres. William McKinley (1843–1901) to protect American citizens in Havana, exploded and sank on February 15, killing 260 men. (LOC, LC-USZ62-103944.)

The Spanish–American War lasted only 113 days, from April 25 until August 12, 1898. As a result of this short war, the United States received Guam, the Philippines, and Puerto Rico from Spain. This is the USS *Maine* entering Havana Harbor in January 1898. (Wikimedia Commons.)

One regiment that deployed from Jefferson Barracks was the Missouri Volunteers, Battery A. The company, encamped on April 26, moved to Jefferson Barracks on May 2 and left on May 16. Its first destination was Chickamauga, Georgia, the site of a major Civil War battle that had claimed many lives and was a Confederate victory. In 1898, troops trained for two months at the camp, which was temporarily renamed Camp Thomas. George H. Thomas (1816–1870), pictured, was a southerner who stayed with the Union during the Civil War. He rose to the rank of major general. An 1840 West Point graduate, Thomas served at Jefferson Barracks in the 2nd Cavalry before the Civil War. (LOC, LC- DIG-cwpbh-00447.)

The conditions were so horrible at Camp Thomas that more men supposedly died there than died in Cuba during the Spanish-American War. This stereograph shows African American soldiers, tent-side, at the Army mobilization camp at Camp Thomas, Chickamauga Park, Georgia, preparing to enter the Spanish-American War. (LOC, LC-USZ62-57440.)

Because the war was short, troops seemed to be in constant movement. The Missouri Volunteers, Battery A, for example, landed in Puerto Rico on August 2, following the US invasion of the island on July 25. The Volunteers sailed back to New York on September 8. Back at Jefferson Barracks on September 18, they were granted 60-day furloughs and mustered out on November 30. Pictured here are troop staff members at Jefferson Barracks in 1898. (Carondelet Historical Society.)

Two Missouri volunteers during the Spanish-American War take advantage of noncombat time to share a letter, perhaps from home. (Carondelet Historical Society.)

Members of the 6th Missouri Volunteers pose for a photograph at Jefferson Barracks during the Spanish-American War. At Jefferson Barracks, they were encamped at Camp Stephens, named for the then governor of Missouri, Lawrence "Lon" Vest Stephens (1855–1923), who served from 1897 to 1901. (Carondelet Historical Society.)

The 6th Missouri Volunteers were stationed in several Cuban cities, including a small town called San Antonio de Banos. The town, located about 20 miles from Havana, was a center for growing tobacco, sugarcane, and pineapples. Soldiers from the 6th Missouri Volunteers are seen here exploring one of the area's caves. (Carondelet Historical Society.)

Col. A. Hardeman, who was earlier stationed at Jefferson Barracks, was affiliated with the barracks again during the Spanish-American War as commander of the 6th Missouri Volunteers. He is pictured here (first row, center) with his staff outside his tent. (Carondelet Historical Society.)

This picture on the left, possibly of Colonel Hardeman, shows him taking time out for a cigar—an item manufactured in San Antonio de Banos at the time. On the right is Colonel Hardeman on horseback at a western post. (Left, Carondelet Historical Society; right, Marc Kollbaum.)

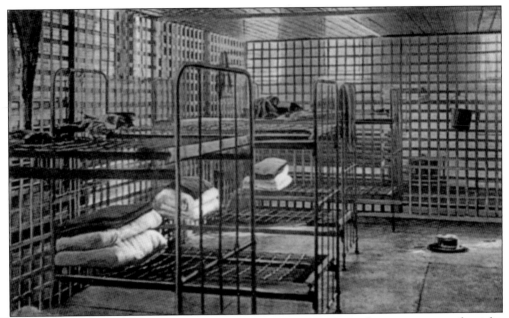

In 1889, Frank E. Woodward, a reporter for the *St. Louis Post-Dispatch*, wrote a series of articles about deplorable conditions at Jefferson Barracks. The buildings were in an advanced state of deterioration. After the troops returned from the war, and Jefferson Barracks was removed as a rendezvous point, the barracks marched head-on into its newest fight—rebuilding the installation. One of the new structures is the guardhouse. This is the interior view of the prisoners' quarters. It remained much the same through the close of World War II. (Carondelet Historical Society.)

The guardhouse was used for infractions by enlisted men and other service members. Political prisoners and prisoners of war were held elsewhere. This photograph is from the early 1900s. (Carondelet Historical Society.)

The post hospital, seen in this 1942 postcard, also underwent changes during that time period. The new hospital was constructed of brick, as were most of the other new-generation buildings on the post. Limestone buildings on the post began to disappear. (Marc Kollbaum.)

One of the major tasks at the barracks was feeding the troops and military personnel. Atkinson Hall, named for the first base commander, could feed 4,000 at a time. (Marc Kollbaum.)

One of the tricks to feeding an army of people was preparedness. The tables were preset for the meal, as seen in this 1909 photograph. (Marc Kollbaum.)

Post. Kitchen and Mess Hall Jefferson . Barracks. Mo.

It was imperative to feed the troops in a timely manner. For the kitchen, that meant a large staff and even larger equipment. (Marc Kollbaum.)

The Jefferson Barracks Post Exchange and Gymnasium building was part of the second phase of this new building project. Designed in 1902 and built in 1905, it served as an activities and recreation center for soldiers. The main room of the gymnasium featured an inside track on the second floor. The building is now the site of the Missouri Civil War Museum. (Marc Kollbaum.)

These Jefferson Barracks duplexes were living quarters known as Officers' Row. They faced the parade grounds. While not all of the buildings that once occupied this section of Hancock Road remain, some of them have enjoyed new life recently. For instance, one of the duplex buildings is now occupied by the AT&T Telephone Pioneers. (Marc Kollbaum.)

Commanding Officer's Quarters. Jefferson Barracks, Mo.

Building Seven, the commanding officer's quarters, was part of the renovation program of the decade. (Marc Kollbaum.)

This postcard shows some of the busiest buildings on the post. From left to right are the post office, gymnasium, post exchange, and streetcar station. This photograph is from the early 1930s. (Marc Kollbaum.)

The Southern Electric Railroad Company was the trolley, or streetcar, system that operated at Jefferson Barracks. Opening day saw over 66,000 riders to Jefferson Barracks. It was the largest single day of fares for the company, which ran its electric cars all day. The fare was probably a nickel. The US post office used the streetcar system, which was inaugurated in Jefferson Barracks between 1896 and 1898. This photograph above is from 1902. The 1898 photograph below shows a crowded trolley near the trolley depot. Although this photograph is posed, the trolley was often overcrowded, as Jefferson Barracks was a popular destination for residents of the St. Louis metropolitan area. Members of the Missouri Volunteers, Battery A, pose with other riders in this image. (Above, Marc Kollbaum; below, Carondelet Historical Society.)

The headquarters, or Administration Building, the structure nearest the Mississippi River, was completed in 1900. Like most buildings, it was designed with both a front and rear elevation, with emphasis on the front. But because the side facing the river was deemed as important as that facing the military post, the plans were changed and the building constructed with two identical front sides. (Marc Kollbaum.)

One spoil of the Spanish-American War found a permanent home at Jefferson Barracks. On July 3, 1898, the Spanish battleship *Oquenda* was sunk in Santiago Bay, Cuba. One of its cannon was retrieved from the wreckage and presented to Jefferson Barracks in August 1899. More than a century later, it still stands—a sturdy symbol of the first eight decades of Jefferson Barracks' history. (Marc Kollbaum.)

Five

A PERIOD OF PEACE

A large number of events took place on the barracks campus, mostly on the parade grounds. A crowd has gathered around the flagpole in this early photograph, which is dated from 1898 to 1904. (Carondelet Historical Society.)

The Grand Army of the Republic (GAR), a fraternal organization of Union army veterans, was founded in Decatur, Illinois, the year following the Civil War. Unusual at the time, both African American and white veterans were encouraged to join. The group also advocated voting rights for African American veterans. After a dip in popularity, GAR membership reached its peak in the 1890s. The national organization held an annual encampment at different locations in the United States. The 1898 encampment, pictured on this page, was held at Jefferson Barracks. The group declined in the 20th century, folding in 1956 when its last member passed away. (Both, Carondelet Historical Society.)

The trolley was usually busy with passengers between St. Louis and Jefferson Barracks. This picture shows the trolley (streetcar) depot at Jefferson Barracks. Along with traveling soldiers, three men in the right foreground appear to be on guard duty, which was standard at the depot. (Marc Kollbaum.)

Jefferson Barracks was the site for many community events. This band concert was held on the parade grounds in 1900 for soldiers and the public. This image shows ladies and gents arriving in the finery of the era. The band is playing in the gazebo. (Marc Kollbaum.)

Because St. Louis held such a significant role in the 19th century's march west, both in peace and war, it was of little surprise it would become the destination, rather than the launching point, for one of the largest endeavors in American history—the Louisiana Purchase Exposition. The fair's dedication on April 30, 1903, was 100 years to the day after the signing of the Louisiana Purchase Treaty, ratified in October 1803. The momentous anniversary brought together three presidents. Pictured, from left to right, are Grover Cleveland (1837–1908), the 22nd president from 1885 to 1889 and 24th president from 1893 to 1897; Pres. Theodore Roosevelt (1858–1919), who had been the 25th vice president under William McKinley but, after six months, assumed the presidency after McKinley's assassination on September 14, 1901; and David Rowland Francis (1850–1927), who was president of the Louisiana Purchase Exposition and had been the 26th mayor of St. Louis from 1885 to 1889 as well as the 27th governor of Missouri from 1889 to 1893. Francis was named US Secretary of the Interior from 1896 to 1897 by President Cleveland. Both houses of Congress, the Supreme Court, the Cabinet, most state governors, and most foreign ministers in the United States were also present for the dedication. Here, the presidents are leaving David Francis' house to participate in the ceremonies. (LOC, LC-USZ62-104953.)

After early construction delays, it was apparent that the fair would not be ready to open on the true centennial. Dedication Day served as a preview for the fair, which opened on April 30, 1904. President Theodore Roosevelt, unable to attend, sent his secretary of war, William Howard Taft (1857–1930), as his representative. Roosevelt made an official appearance at the exposition as the guest of honor on President's Day, November 27, 1904. Among the fair's exhibits were those from Puerto Rico, Guam, and the Philippines—areas acquired by the United States in the Spanish-American War. Military parades were daily events during the fair. Each day had a theme, and most had special guests. Jefferson Barracks troops were a daily presence. Below, the cavalry from Jefferson Barracks leads a parade. Over 20 million people attended the fair from April 30, 1904, until it closed on December 1. (Both, Marc Kollbaum.)

Unlike most military dignitaries who started their military careers at Jefferson Barracks after graduating from West Point, Dwight "Ike" David Eisenhower (1890–1969) began his military career at Jefferson Barracks: Eisenhower spent days at Jefferson Barracks taking his first entrance exams for West Point, where he became a cadet in 1911. After graduation in 1915, Ike returned to his native Texas for service. He went on to become an officer of the newly formed tank corps during World War I. His major military fame, though, came during World War II. Already a five-star general, Eisenhower was promoted to the rank of Supreme Allied Commander in Europe. Besides numerous American awards and medals, Eisenhower received commendations from at least 30 foreign countries. Following the war, he became president of Columbia University from 1948 to 1953 and the 34th president of the United States from 1953 to 1961. (Carondelet Historical Society.)

On March 1, 1912, Army Capt. Albert "Bert" Berry and pilot Antony "Tony" Habersack Jannus (1889–1916) took off from Kinloch Air Field (now Lambert-St. Louis International Airport) and flew the 17 miles south to Jefferson Barracks at an approximate height of 1,500 feet. Their plane was a Benoist Type XII. They were about to accomplish the first parachute drop from an airplane. The parachute, hidden in the cone in the front of the plane, contained no harness. In the inset on the lower left, Berry sits on a trapeze bar connected to suspension lines during his descent. Berry landed on the parade grounds to the cheers and applause of hundreds of spectators. It is significant that the first parachute jump occurred at Jefferson Barracks because the military and politicians were interested in using this method for future combat details. (Carondelet Historical Society.)

AERO
AMERICA'S
AVIATION WEEKLY

March 9, 1912   TEN CENTS   Vol. III No. 23

The 1912 parachute jump received national attention, including placement on the cover of *AERO*, a top weekly flight magazine of the era, on March 5, 1912. Tony Jannus died in Russia in 1916 when the airplane he was piloting crashed over the Black Sea while he was training two of Tsar Nikolai Romanov's men as pilots. Jannus's body was never found. In 1964, the Tony Jannus Distinguished Aviation Society was established. The Florida-based organization presents yearly awards to distinguished aviators. (Carondelet Historical Society.)

Charles A. Lindbergh (1902–1974), an American aviation pioneer, was inducted into the 110th Flying Squadron, Army Air Corps National Guard at Jefferson Barracks. Several years later, as he flew the *Spirit of St. Louis* across the Atlantic and into international history, a patch on the side of his plane showed a kicking mule—the mascot of his Missouri squadron. The letter below was sent on May 21, 1927, and requested a cablegram be sent to Lindbergh, assuring him that his comrades flew with him in spirit "every inch of the way." (Right, LOC, LC-B2-5897-15; below, National Archives, Bryan McGraw.)

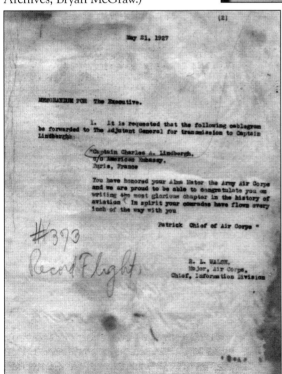

The keynote to most parades and events is good music. Jefferson Barracks, over the years, has been the home of many bands. This is the 3rd US Cavalry Band at Jefferson Barracks. The photograph is dated between 1894 and 1898. (Marc Kollbaum.)

This band, shown posed on the parade grounds, is the US Cavalry Band. The photograph dates from 1894 to 1898. The band definitely reflects the true nature of the cavalry by playing on horseback. (Marc Kollbaum.)

UNITED STATES DEPOT BAND, JEFFERSON BARRACKS, MO.

MR. C. G. CONN,
           I congratulate you upon the great work you have done for musicians and for your untiring efforts to supply Army musicians with Instruments that makes their work both pleasant and efficient.   FRANK J. WEBER, Bandmaster.

At the turn of the 20th century, military music was extremely popular. By then, John Phillip Sousa (1854–1932) had already written "Semper Fidelis" (the Marine Corps march), "The Washington Post," "The Liberty Bell," and "Stars and Stripes Forever," the official national march of the United States. Over his long career, Sousa wrote 136 marches. Above, the US Depot Band was under the direction of bandmaster Frank J. Weber when this photograph was taken in 1907. Below, the 6th Infantry Band is sitting in front of the band barracks, Building 66. The two-story structure, still standing on the installation, was one of the new constructions of the 1890s. The only band members whose names are known are those seated in the first row—Warrant Officer Lewis (left) and Sgt. Karl Schmidt. (Both, Marc Kollbaum.)

Parade Day, Jefferson Barracks, St. Louis, Mo.

This photograph of Parade Day in 1914 also highlights the parade grounds. Several months before this was taken, on January 10, 1914, the ongoing Mexican Revolution accelerated. Pancho Villa and his men overtook the town of Ojinaga in Chihuahua, Mexico. The United States remained neutral militarily until Pres. Woodrow Wilson (1856–1924), the 28th president of the United States from 1913 to 1921, ordered troops to be sent to Mexico in 1914. (Marc Kollbaum.)

Deployment of American troops to Mexico continued. Gen. John J. "Black Jack" Pershing was sent to Mexico in an unsuccessful attempt to capture Pancho Villa. Despite the duration of the conflict, America never declared war against Mexico or any of the factions. Here, soldiers are leaving Jefferson Barracks for Mexico, for an operation called the Mexican Punitive Expedition. (Marc Kollbaum.)

84

Six

THE FIRST WORLD WAR

In 1914, tensions were also accelerating in Europe. The European war started in earnest in June 1914 with the Serbian assassination of Archduke Franz Ferdinand (1863–1914) in Sarajevo. Ferdinand was by then the heir-apparent to the Austro-Hungarian throne. His death began the war between Serbia and it allies and Austria-Hungary, Germany, and the Ottoman Empire. Pres. Woodrow Wilson resisted joining the fracas. But by the time of his second inauguration in March 1917, Wilson, who is pictured here with his wife, Edith Bolling Galt (1872–1961), was but a few weeks away from sending troops on April 6, 1917. (LOC, LC-USZ62-22737.)

Recruits enlisted and remained at Jefferson Barracks. The largest single day for enlistment at the barracks saw over 3,000 recruits. Eventually, potential troops, at times, were turned away. Here, men are lined up waiting to enlist. (Carondelet Historical Society.)

After signing up, new recruits go in another line to receive their Army issue. (Carondelet Historical Society.)

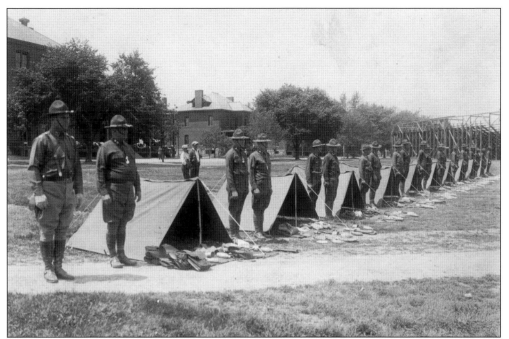

These recruits are standing alongside their Army pup tents. From left to right (the men are identified on the back of the picture) are First Sergeant Moundy, Corporal Bickmure, Taylor G. Phelix, Cap Wilson, Turner Coaty, Bob Gannon, Edgar Rigs, Fred Rigs, Speedy Stuart, George D., Mitchel S., and George Seal. (Carondelet Historical Society.)

Jefferson Barracks became one of the largest induction and mustering out centers in the United States during World War I, titles it would retain through the end of World War II. Because of the number of inductions, space at the barracks was at a premium. By December 1917, over 12,000 recruits were on base, setting a record. Tent cities appeared in various places on the complex, like this one on the parade grounds, which was photographed in May 1918. (Marc Kollbaum.)

Large numbers of soldiers deployed at a time. Here, men are waiting on the hillside above the train depot for their turn to board the train for shipment abroad. The Administration Building is visible in the left corner of the photograph. (Carondelet Historical Society.)

Even when the troop train arrived for departure, embarking on their journey required waiting in more long lines, as seen in this 1918 photograph. (Carondelet Historical Society.)

The troops at Jefferson Barracks, like these pictured here in 1918, continued to form on the parade grounds for their traditional parades and military reviews. (Marc Kollbaum.)

A group of World War I soldiers poses at Jefferson Barracks. Their tents are seen in the far left. (Carondelet Historical Society, Cyrill Drozda Collection.)

Along with daily activities and formal ceremonies continuing during the war, the troops also trained in combat strategies and tactics on the Jefferson Barracks complex before deployment overseas. (Marc Kollbaum.)

Pictured are the 1917 staff and officers of Jefferson Barracks. (Carondelet Historical Society.)

Crews and their tanks trained on the fields of Jefferson Barracks. (Carondelet Historical Society, Cyrill Drozda Collection.)

New recruits at Jefferson Barracks in 1917 are gathered around a sergeant, who is giving them instructions on hygiene and conduct before their deployments. (Carondelet Historical Society.)

Walter Short (1880–1949) began his military career in 1916 with the search for Pancho Villa in Mexico. He participated in World War I (pictured left), was stationed at Jefferson Barracks in the 1930s as an officer in the 6th Infantry, and became barracks commander. Short was the commanding Army officer in Hawaii during the attack on Pearl Harbor on December 7, 1941. Blamed for the intensity of the attack, he was relieved of his command on December 17 and reduced from the rank of lieutenant general to major general. Congress posthumously exonerated him on May 25, 1999, but his rank was not restored. (Both, Carondelet Historical Society.)

John J. "Black Jack" Pershing (1860–1948), a native Missourian, was born in Laclede in Linn County. His father, John F., was a sutler for the 18th Missouri Volunteer Infantry in the Civil War. John J. was an 1886 West Point graduate. There, he was noticed for strong leadership qualities. He commanded the cadet guard at the funeral of Ulysses S. Grant. Pershing is the only living person to receive the highest rank in the Army—General of the Armies of the United States. In December 1919, Pershing visited Jefferson Barracks with his then 10-year-old son, Warren. He reviewed the troops and visited the sick and wounded, many of whom were still recuperating from their war wounds. (LOC, LC-DIG-hec-07393.)

Maj. Gen. Leonard Wood (1860–1927) was the Army Chief of Staff. He was a friend of Theodore Roosevelt and, with Roosevelt, organized the 1st Volunteer Cavalry, known as the Rough Riders, in the Spanish-American War. A Medal of Honor winner, Wood spent time at Jefferson Barracks in 1920 during his unsuccessful attempt to secure the Republican nomination for president. Fort Leonard Wood in southwest Missouri was established in late 1940 and named after Wood in early 1941. (LOC, LC-DIG-ggbain-24085.)

As the Roaring Twenties emerged, peace had returned to America. The men in this picture, members of the rifle team of 1921, had the time to train and hone their skills to win this trophy. (Marc Kollbaum.)

In 1922, the Citizens' Military Training Camps (CMTC) for young men came to Jefferson Barracks, guided by the National Defense Act of 1920. Like regular troops, CMTC soldiers received physical fitness training (PT). The camps met annually in summer. (Marc Kollbaum.)

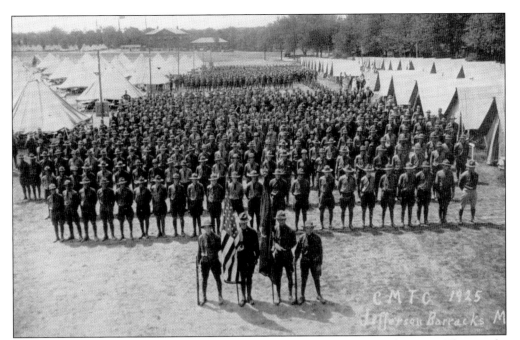

By 1925, when this CMTC photograph was taken, the programs continued to grow. The month-long, live-in program's participants slept in tents, seen here to the rear and sides of the formation. (Marc Kollbaum.)

The programs peaked in 1928 and 1929, when they were held on about 50 bases nationwide. Despite the fact that the men could receive a second lieutenant's commission in the reserves by completing four consecutive summers of CMTC, fewer than anticipated completed those requirements. Participation waned in the 1930s, and the idea of CMTC came to an end with the start of World War II. (Marc Kollbaum.)

In late September 1927, a tornado hit the St. Louis area. Troops from Jefferson Barracks, pictured here, helped with the clean up. Seventy-nine people were killed in this disaster and over 500 were injured. It is considered one of the costliest tornadoes in American history. (Carondelet Historical Society.)

With the stock market crash behind them as 1929 came to an end, Americans prepared to face the uncertainties of the next decade. Officers and their families put aside those thoughts as they celebrate Christmas Day in 1929, together at the headquarters party on the barracks. (Carondelet Historical Society.)

Grooming was not always the top concern in the military. Early troops had no given standards for hair. In the 20th century, however, grooming became a larger matter. By the 1920s, barbershops were standard fixtures on military posts. This photograph shows a Jefferson Barracks barbershop from the late 1920s or early 1930s. Mr. Simmons, the post's head barber, is at the left. (Carondelet Historical Society.)

The post exchange, or PX, was the modern incarnation of the sutler's store. Jefferson Barracks personnel and their families shopped at the barracks store for groceries and general items. (John Maurath.)

Walter Krueger (1881–1967) was born in West Prussia. After his father's death, eight-year-old Walter immigrated to St. Louis with his mother and siblings to be near his mother's uncle. Serving in both the Spanish-American War and World War I, Krueger was commander of the 6th Infantry at Jefferson Barracks from 1932 to 1934. He created an unofficial, covert unit called the Alamo Scouts in 1943. In 1945, he was promoted to four-star general, making him the first Army soldier to rise from the rank of private to general. (Carondelet Historical Society.)

Also in 1934, Jefferson Barracks, under Commander Krueger, participated in an officer exchange program. Pictured on horseback are, from left to right, Walter Krueger, Capt. George O. Vonland, Japanese Exchange Officer Major Tagasaki, and Captain Irwin. Earlier that day, Krueger had presented Captain Vonland, a St. Louis native, the Distinguished Service Cross for his actions on July 6, 1918, in Hilsenfirst, France. This is the second-highest US army decoration. Later in 1934, Krueger's command of Jefferson Barracks was succeeded by Walter Short, who served as base commander from 1934 to 1936. (Carondelet Historical Society.)

The first years of the 1930s saw America in the depths of the Depression. When Franklin Delano Roosevelt (1882–1945) became president on March 4, 1933, he faced a myriad of Depression-related problems. Many programs created during the early years of his unequaled four terms became known collectively as the New Deal. One very successful program was the Civilian Conservation Corps, or CCC. In its early years, the program accepted young men, mostly on relief and from rural areas. (LOC, LC-USZ62-117121.)

Designed to conserve the failing infrastructure, the CCC programs were often established on military bases, as was the Jefferson Barracks CCC program. It became a Congressional-backed program in 1937 and a federal security agency in 1939. The CCC focus shifted from conservation to national defense by the start of 1940. It disappeared during World War II. Jefferson Barracks hosts this bronze statue, located at 16 Hancock Road, just east of the former CCC Museum. Dedicated in 1996, it is the second of more than 50 CCC statues and monuments in the United States. (Carondelet Historical Society.)

The 1930s had been a period of relative peace, although America was coping with struggles caused by the Depression. Because of the calm, numbers of enlisted men continued to decrease, including at Jefferson Barracks. Throughout history, Jefferson Barracks saw periods of great enlistment, especially during wars, as well as times during which the number of new recruits diminished. No one, however, could have imagined that, with the advent of the new decade, America would again become involved in another world war. This picture, from late 1942, shows thousands of troops from Jefferson Barracks as they converge from all directions onto the center of the parade field for review. Many troops are already on the field in formation, while other soldiers are still marching forward to join them. (Marc Kollbaum.)

Seven

THE SECOND WORLD WAR

The 1941 Jefferson Barracks Christmas card was probably mailed and displayed in many households when the world was forever changed on Sunday, December 7, 1941, because of the bombings at Pearl Harbor, Hawaii. The United States, previously attempting to remain neutral, was now engaged in World War II. (Carondelet Historical Society.)

Jefferson Barracks HUB

Volume 4 No. 7 OFFICIAL PUBLICATION OF AIR FORCES BASIC TRAINING CENTER, JEFFERSON BARRACKS, MISSOURI Saturday, February 12, 1944

Post to Have 15 Men in Golden Gloves

War Bond Sales Near $300,000

Grand Total Almost Triple J.B. Goal In Fourth Campaign

Jefferson Barracks' participation in the Fourth War Loan Drive moved into "overwhelming success" brackets this week as a flurry of new purchases rocketed the grand total to $290,241.50, almost triple the Post's goal of $100,000. However, 2nd Lt. Robert G. Lieerman, Post War Bond Officer, reminds all concerned that the campaign is not over until February 29 and J.B. is still shooting for more as "the bigger we do the better."

Although the drive has brought a remarkable response in cash purchases, all-out efforts are urged in the Class B allotment program of regular month-to-month pay deductions for bonds. And it is the expressed desire of Col. Converse R. Lewis, Post Commander, that all military personnel in this Post be enrolled for Class B allotments. Allotments of course, are not counted in War Loan Drive figures.

Standings in the campaign this week show the following organizations over the top: Hq. BTC Officers, Hq. Sq. BTC, the 509th and 510th AAF Bands, 868th Guard Squadron, 14th Wing Detachment, Veterinary Detachment, 1st Mess Group, 84th Aviation Squadron, Finance Office, 862nd Signal Service Company, 811th and 932nd Quartermaster units, Quartermaster Detachment, and the 25th, 28th, 31st, 23rd, 24th, 33rd, 32nd, 718th, 707th, 27th, 29th, 35th, 36th, 1168th and 1167th training groups. The 14th Wing is the only wing thus far with all its training groups plus the wing detachment over the top.

Big Sale

Among the civilian organizations, Miscellaneous Administration, the Motor Pool and the Post Exchange employes have topped their goals. Added momentum was given the (Continued on Page 8)

31st Moves to Top In Singing Parade

The 31st Training Group's singing spirit, which has been soaring mightily for the past several weeks, surged to the head of the list this week by taking top honors in the Post singing competition. The winning laurels climaxed consecutive runner-up honors for the 31st last week and the week before.

The 22nd Training Group of the 13th Wing took the week's runner-up honors. Singing is carried on here during all marching formations and during physical training periods. Post song sheets are used daily.

Mr. John T. Bailey, Post Morale Singing Officer, also hands out a special commendation to the 23rd Training Group of the 13th Wing for continuing the fine work that put the group in the top spot last week. Going full speed ahead, each squadron in the 23rd is now planning to organize its own glee club.

Disney Did It for J.B.

This fast-flying bee, forming the letter "J" as he buzzes through the air, was drawn by the famed movie cartoonist, Walt Disney, as the official insigne of Jefferson Barracks. Disney created the insigne at the request of Maj. Henry W. Webb, Post Public Relations Officer.

J.B. Legal Office Will Help You Prepare Income Tax Returns

That time is drawing near again. March 15, the deadline for filing 1943 income tax returns is not far off, and although there are very few men in service who will have to pay any taxes on their incomes, there are many who must file returns. As a matter of fact, because of refund provisions in the new income tax law if a service man had all or any part of his taxes last year it is definitely to his advantage to file a return this year. For in 90 per cent of such cases there'll be refunds.

Although the HUB has no intentions of getting very technical about income tax procedure, thereby confusing both ourselves and our readers, the Post Legal Officer comes forth with the following advice on the problem as it concerns J.B. personnel:

All military personnel at this station may obtain assistance in the preparation of their 1943 Federal and State income tax returns from specially trained men in their respective organizations. These men have been trained by the Post Legal Office in co-operation with the Office of the Collector of Internal Revenue in St. Louis. Their names and the time and place available may be ascertained at the headquarters of the various organizations on the Post.

This Is Needed

Those desiring assistance should first obtain the following information:

Exact figures on 1943 income and deductions; exact figures on 1942 income and deductions; copy of 1942 return, if available; copy of U. S. Treasury Form 1125 (Statement of 1942 Federal Income tax and payments thereon); statement of victory

Riviera Club Show To Be Here Tuesday

Woody Wilson and his orchestra plus the complete floor show from the Riviera Club, popular St. Louis night spot, will entertain J.B. GIs Tuesday night with a variety-spiced program at the Tent Arena. Curtain time is 8 p. m.

The show, brought here by the Post Special Service Office, features Lischeron and Adams, sensational dance team; Kay Hughes, song stylist, and Mel Cardo, magician.

Fighters Ready for Downtown Tournament Starting Monday

Starting Monday night, the Globe-Democrat Golden Gloves tournament—staged in Kiel Auditorium—will afford our Jay Bee punchers an opportunity to test their Sunday pokes on non-G.I. chins as well as the variety they are ordinarily accustomed to. For with a great number of teams entered from St. Louis and the surrounding area, competition promises to be rugged. And with the last-minute entrance of the Keesler Field, Miss., squad, the show takes on almost a national flavor.

Jefferson Barracks will send a 15-man team downtown, composed of both Post Golden Gloves champs and outstanding contenders in the recently concluded HUB tourney. Many of the lads who lost out along the way are really top-notch scrappers, and because of this they will have the opportunity to again demonstrate their fistic wares.

Col. Converse R. Lewis, Post commander, is solidly behind his boys, and will be on hand when they square off on the firing line Monday. Here is the team:

NOVICE CLASS: 126 pounds—Harold Toshner, 22nd; 147 pounds—Norman McCann, 22nd; 160 pounds —Weldon Beyer, 1167th, James Hollis, 1168th, and Alvin Scott, 1168th. 175 pounds—Bill McCoy, 26th, and John W. Evans, 1167th. Heavyweight—Eugene Gaciley, 1168th.

Watch Sammy

OPEN CLASS: 126 pounds—Darrell Whitsell, Mess Squadron; 135-pounds—Sammy Schipani, Hq. Sq.; 147 pounds—Ed Webb, 1165th; 160 pounds—Russell Flynn, Medics; 175 pounds—Lucien Taliaferro, Jr., 932nd Q. M.; Heavyweight—Bill Jackson, 1167th, and Robert Sherrill, 932nd Q. M.

There they are, the Jay Bee jabbers. And they really earned it. Few tournaments ever featured as many knockouts as were seen in the HUB's three-day tourney. The staggering total of 27 kayoes were registered in 46 bouts, well over 50 percent of the lads being put away via the slumber route. This is an unprecedented proportion, inasmuch as most amateur fights are decided by decision, and it serves as a advance warning that the opponents in Kiel Auditorium are in for a rough evening Monday.

Most of the Jay Bee strength is concentrated in the 160 and 175 pound classes, but the other weights are represented by able boys who can take care of themselves. Sammy Schipani, 135-pound open champ, is expected, among others, to go a long, long way. The popu- (Continued on Page 8)

Radio Schedule Includes Two Big Programs on Post

Weekend radio highlights, including the network appearance of a Jefferson Barracks radio-operator gunner, include two on-post broadcasts. "Accent on Wings" (KSD—2 p. m. Saturday) and "Soldiers at Worship" (KWK—11:05 a. m. Sunday).

This afternoon's "Accent on Wings," 13th in the KSD series, will feature the interview appearance of a combat veteran, varied musical emphasis by the Military Band and Jive Boosters orchestra. The band, under CWO Bennie Maniscalco's direction, will play a Cpl. Art Hill's arrangement of "Brazil," "Perpetual Motion," "Them Bass" and "Chinese Temple Garden." Dance orchestra selections include "Rose Room," as arranged by S/Sgt. Paul Stanis, and "The Bounce." The Bombers will be directed by T/Sgt. Jimmy Lamont.

"Soldiers at Worship" Sunday morning, continuing with a variation of denominational services as held on the Post, will be an Afro-Methodist program. "Gratitude and Courage" is the subject of Chaplain L. A. Stroud's sermon, while a choir of Negro soldier voices will provide music. The KWK program originates from Chapel No. 3. Part of the service will be dedicated to the memory of Abraham Lincoln.

Col. Lewis Mails Valentine to Tot Who Sent Him One

Hazel Croft, the eight-year-old girl in Goshen, Nova Scotia, who received a teddy bear and other Christmas gifts from Col. Converse R. Lewis, commanding officer, and men of the Public Relations office at Jefferson Barracks last Christmas, remembered her American soldier friends this week—with a valentine.

The valentine from the little Canadian girl was addressed to the post commander, and was accompanied by a penciled letter in which she said she had been sick in bed for a month "but I ain't alone in bed. I got my teddy with me."

Hazel tied a Santa Claus note to a Christmas tree cut down near her home, which eventually found its way to Service Club No. 1. The Jefferson Barracks soldiers in reply sent a Christmas package, including not only the teddy bear she asked for but other toys and goodies, on a 3000-mile journey to her.

Hazel will soon receive another surprise, for Colonel Lewis, upon receipt of her Valentine greetings, has sent her a huge valentine in return which was drawn specially for her by Pvt. Ralph B. Olian, Public Relations staff artist.

Pappy Cheshire and Gang to Be at Tent Arena Thursday

Pappy Cheshire and His Gang, popular entertainers from Radio Station KMOX in St. Louis, will bring their hillbilly songs and antics to the Tent Arena Thursday eve as a Post Special Service Office feature. Curtain time will be 7:45 p. m.

Long featured on the air, Cheshire and his crew have gained national fame by appearances on the Nation's Ad Dance program and by making several movies out Hollywood way.

Stars of the show include Skeets, the Golden Voiced Yodeler; lovely Sally Foster, known as "the girl with a smile in her voice;" Wade Ray, Roy Fields, Delph Hewitt, Bob Hasting and Slim Bland.

Celebrities did much for the war effort during World War II. During the war, Jefferson Barracks was visited by many of the top stars in the nation. Bob Hope (1903–2003) began his famous United Service Organizations (USO) shows in May 1941. He visited Jefferson Barracks on occasion, also bringing friends like comedian Jerry Colonna (1904–1986) and singer Frances Langford (1914 –2005). Judy Garland (1922–1969) also entertained the troops at Jefferson Barracks. One distinct Hollywood presence during the World War II years was a drawing by Missouri native Walt Disney, who created the "J Bee" specifically for Jefferson Barracks. This unique design is seen here in an edition of the *Hub* newspaper. (Marc Kollbaum.)

A patriotic push of the World War II period was the purchase of war bonds. The idea was not new: bonds to help finance war were sold by both sides in the Civil War. The World War I campaigns to sell Liberty bonds were successful, promoted by celebrities of the day. Following Pearl Harbor, the name of bonds changed to war bonds. For World War II, celebrities were again used to promote bonds. Stamps could be bought at ten-cent intervals and placed in an approved album until the bond price was raised. In this photograph, taken at Jefferson Barracks during World War II, troops are participating in a war bond purchasing effort. (Carondelet Historical Society.)

World War II saw the creation of the Women's Army Auxiliary Corps (WAACs). Here, the women of the squad are standing in formation for review in this photograph taken on the parade grounds around 1943. (Marc Kollbaum.)

Howard Rusk (1901–1989), a prominent St. Louis physician, enlisted shortly after Pearl Harbor. While attached to the barracks in 1942, Rusk noticed a lack of significant programs to help rehabilitate the wounded, mostly members of the Army Air Corps in the post hospital. He became the founder of rehabilitative medicine. Rusk was moved from Jefferson Barracks in early 1943 to the Pentagon to expand his findings nationwide. Rusk's dedication to his field garnered him many awards, as well as the nickname, "Doctor Live-Again." Above, Colonel Rusk (second from the left) and movie star Cary Grant (center) pose with others in February 1945 at the Army Air Forces Convalescent Hospital in Florida. Pictured below is one of the rehabilitation classes at Jefferson Barracks in 1942. (Both, Western Collection, University of Missouri–St. Louis Library Archives.)

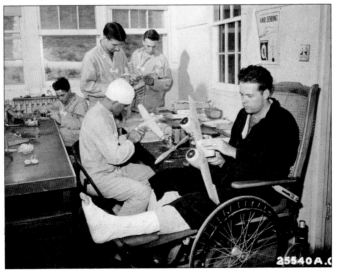

Jefferson Barracks was, again, one of the largest induction centers in the United States. Many temporary buildings were constructed. One of them was a two-story induction center, which was on the north side of the post. Pictured here, in front of that structure, is the 28th training group around 1944. (Marc Kollbaum.)

Patriotism was high during the war, with everyone trying to do his or her part. Friends and family from the St. Louis area would often accompany their friends to Jefferson Barracks as they enlisted or deployed. This group of friends from the Maplewood area, seen here on part of the 1851 limestone wall, made the trip to Jefferson Barracks numerous times to see their friends off or welcome them home. Pictured, from left to right, are Jeanette Callaway Foley, the author's aunt; Velda Callaway Smith, the author's mother; and three of their friends. (Joseph J. Grassino.)

The barracks housed both German and Italian prisoners of war during this time. Often, the Italian prisoners would be allowed to take a bus to The Hill, the Italian section of St. Louis, to attend Catholic mass on Sundays. Since a large number of young men who would normally do the laborers' jobs in the area were away at war, the prisoners of war were often used for work they were accustomed to. Sometimes, they were transported miles away to work in the wine areas in mid-Missouri. A German prisoner of war claimed authorship of this swastika carved into the limestone wall near the Spanish-American cannon. (Art Schuermann.)

Pres. Franklin D. Roosevelt came to Jefferson Barracks in 1943 to review the troops. His wife, Eleanor, is seated in the automobile next to him. When Roosevelt made this trip to the barracks, the length of the war and its outcome were still in question. Roosevelt, through his four terms in office, led the country through both the Depression and the Second World War. He died April 12, 1945—mere months before the war ended. (Marc Kollbaum.)

Eight

DECOMISSION AND TODAY

In 1946, with World War II over, the government severely downsized its holdings. Jefferson Barracks was among the properties designated as surplus and unnecessary. Decommissioned as an active installation, the post remained open as a Missouri Air National Guard installation. The above list of post commanders stops at the time of decommission. (Art Schuermann.)

Thurs, July 21, 1966 - St. Louis Post Dispatch

By a Post-Dispatch Photographer

Resting After Fighting Fire Nine Hours

Lemay firemen resting after working nearly nine hours to extinguish a fire that damaged a three-story brick building opposite the old parade ground at Jefferson Barracks Tuesday. The building, No. 11, was occupied by Communications Squadrons 218 and 266 of the Missouri Air National Guard, who are on annual summer encampment. The firemen are (from left) Don Schorage, Thomas Thomas, Capt. Emil Mueller (front, with boots off) and Joe Valentine.

Building Eleven was damaged by fire on July 20, 1966. The three-story structure was occupied by the Air National Guard's Communications Squadrons 218 and 219, as identified in this newspaper article from the *St. Louis Post-Dispatch*, which was printed the next day. The article also identifies the firemen as, from left to right, Don Schorage, Thomas Thomas, Capt. Emil Mueller, and Joe Valentine. The picture below is identified as an evidential photograph from December 1966. (Both, Carondelet Historical Society.)

EXHIBIT "B" R/S 7 Dec 1966
119,341.55, MoANG, Jeff Bk

An entire Air National Guard unit from the 1970s at Jefferson Barracks is pictured here. (Carondelet Historical Society.)

Troops here are engaged in a close order drill at the barracks. (Carondelet Historical Society.)

Post Theater, Jefferson Barracks, Mo.

While the drills and activities continued, many of the buildings on the post were no longer needed. The Jefferson Barracks theater, which showed movies weekly during the 1930s and 1940s, became part of the St. Bernadette Catholic Church complex after the post's decommission. (Marc Kollbaum.)

This former barracks hospital became part of Mehlville School District. First used by the district as a school, it is now home to offices. (Marc Kollbaum.)

Here, the former barn, near the Laborers' House, is seen during renovation. It is currently the visitor center for Jefferson Barracks. Meetings are held here, and it also houses the gift shop. (Marc Kollbaum.)

Pictured here is the current renovated visitor center at Jefferson Barracks. (Art Schuermann.)

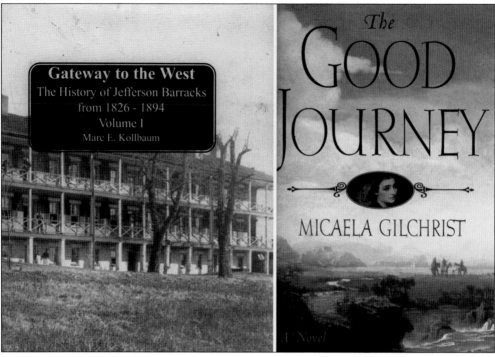

Many refuse to let the rich, vivid history associated with Jefferson Barracks be forgotten. Numerous books about or relating to the barracks have been written in recent years. Among them is the first volume of the history of Jefferson Barracks by Marc Kollbaum, which is shown at the left. On the right is a historical novel, *The Good Journey*, by Micaela Gilchrist, which chronicles the first years of the military installation as seen through the eyes of Mary Bullitt Atkinson, the wife of the first post commander. (Left, Marc Kollbaum; right, Micaela Gilchrist.)

One of the more noticeable objects on the post is at the entrance to the military installation. An F-4 Phantom, this plane bears the Air Force pattern that was used on these aircraft during the Vietnam War. On the right, this recent photograph of a Missouri Guard Apache attack helicopter, flying above the Mississippi River, also shows a more modern aerial view of the current Jefferson Barracks. (Left, Art Schuermann; right, Jefferson Barracks Heritage Foundation, Bill Florich.)

Nine

SOME GAVE ALL

This 1913 postcard shows soldiers removing a fellow soldier from a building on the barracks for his final trip on a horse-drawn hearse for burial at the national cemetery. (Marc Kollbaum.)

Three Revolutionary War patriots are buried at Jefferson Barracks National Cemetery. The three are Thomas Hunt, whose grave is pictured here, Russell Bissell, and Richard Gentry. Hunt, who passed away in 1808, remained in the Army after the revolution, advancing to the rank of colonel. Bissell, who died in 1807, was a major and the last commandant of Fort Bellefontaine. Gentry (1763–1843) was present at the capture of Cornwallis at Yorktown. (Connie Nisinger.)

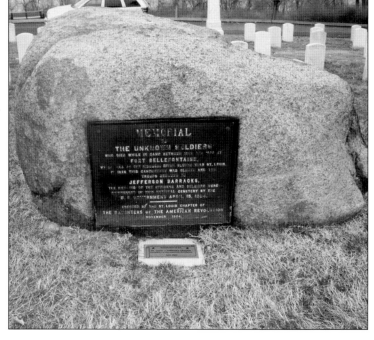

In the early 20th century, the Daughters of the American Revolution (DAR) erected this monument in the national cemetery. Remains of those buried at Fort Bellefontaine were removed and reinterred at Jefferson Barracks at that time. (Connie Nisinger.)

There are eight Medal of Honor recipients interred at the national cemetery. German-born Martin Schubert (1838–1912) was a private in New York's 14th Artillery, Company C, in the Civil War. He received a Medal of Honor for his actions on December 13, 1861, at Fredericksburg, Virginia. (Connie Nisinger.)

Lorenzo Dow Immell (1837–1912) received a Medal of Honor for heroic actions as a corporal in the Battle of Wilson's Creek in 1861. (Left, Carondelet Historical Society; right, Connie Nisinger.)

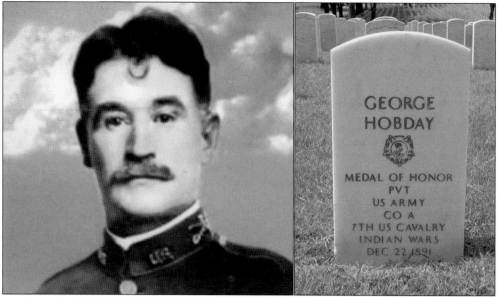

George Hobday, who died in 1891, was a veteran of the Indian Wars. He received his medal for bravery in the Action at Wounded Knee Creek on December 29, 1890. He was serving at the St. Louis Powder Depot at the time of his death from double pneumonia in October 1891. (Left, Wikimedia Commons; right, Connie Nisinger.)

Pictured are the headstones for Alonzo Stokes, who died in 1876, and David Ryan; both also received their Medals of Honor for their deeds during the Indian Wars. A sergeant in the 6th Cavalry, Stokes was awarded for gallantry on July 12, 1870, during the Battle of the Little Wichita River in Texas. Ryan, who died in 1896, was born in Ireland and received his medal for gallantry between October 1876 and January 1877 for actions against the Indians in Cedar Creek, Montana. (Both, Connie Nisinger.)

FREDERICK C BARKER JR AMM3 USN
CHARLES D LINZMEYER ACOM USN
CHARLES A MARTINELLI AMM2 USNR
HERSCHEL A OEHLERT JR LTJG USNR
JOHNNY A RENNER ACRM USN
BRUCE A VAN VOORHIS LCDR USN

JULY 6 1943   279

79 279-280-281

BRUCE A VAN VOORHIS
MEDAL OF HONOR
LCDR US NAVY
JAN 29 1908   JUL 6 1943

Bruce Avery Van Voorhis (1908–1943) is the first of the cemetery's World War II Medal of Honor recipients. He died on July 6, 1943. Awarded his medal posthumously for actions beyond the call of duty, Voorhis was a lieutenant commander in the US Navy, commanding a patrol bomber plane during the Battle of the Solomon Islands. Knowing he would not return safely, he delivered six attacks, destroying much of the enemy's supplies, munitions, and a radio station before crashing under enemy fire. (Art Schuermann.)

CHELI MAJ AC   FREDERICK K KOEBIG
MARCH 6 1944

78   930

RALPH CHELI
MEDAL OF HONOR
MAJ ARMY AIR FORCES
WORLD WAR II
MAR 6 1944

Ralph Cheli, who died on March 6, 1944, was also awarded his medal posthumously for gallantry surrounding his final flight. Major Cheli perished with his crew in Wewak, New Guinea. While he led his squadron, enemy planes focused their attack on his plane, and it burst into flames. Rather than gaining altitude, which would have enabled his men to parachute to safety but would have also disoriented the other planes in his squadron, he made the supreme sacrifice by choosing to continue leading the attack. The target was eliminated. Cheli shifted command to his wingman and crashed his burning plane into the sea. (Connie Nisinger.)

HERSCHEL K DEVORE S SGT
ILAS B DYE T SGT
LEON FOURENS S SGT
LAWRENCE L HOOD S SGT
DONALD D PUCKET 1ST LT
JACK C RATHBUN S SGT
AIR CORPS
JULY 9 1944   270

84 270

DONALD D PUCKET
MEDAL OF HONOR
1LT US ARMY AIR CORPS
WORLD WAR II
JUL 9 1944

Donald Pucket, who died on July 9, 1944, was also awarded his medal posthumously for actions on his final mission. A first lieutenant in the 98th Bombardment group, his plane received heavy damage over Romania shortly after completing a successful attack. At least six crew members, including Ralph Cheli, were killed; others were severely wounded. With his plane filling with gas and out of control, Pucket urged the crew to jump. Three petrified crew members would not leave, and Pucket would not abandon them. The plane crashed into a mountainside. Pucket is part of the mass-grave memorial commemorating the fallen. (Connie Nisinger.)

This memorial obelisk was placed in the national cemetery in 1938. In August 1866, 175 members of the US Colored Infantry died of cholera. Their remains were placed in a "quarantine station" somewhere in Missouri until the move to Jefferson Barracks in 1938. (Connie Nisinger.)

There were no rules and regulations regarding tombstone style and placement until later in the cemetery's history. This photograph shows a wide array of headstones and memorials. (LOC, HABSMO, 1938–3.)

This is one of the earliest group monuments in the cemetery. The soldiers were killed in the Seminole Wars at the Battle of Okeechobee, Florida, on December 25, 1837. Col. Richard Gentry, mentioned here, is not the same one who was a Revolutionary War patriot. (Connie Nisinger.)

John Lyden (left) was in the Confederate army. He was a fireman on a Mississippi gunboat, *The Star of the West*. Confederates were given burial in the cemetery, but their headstones all come to a point on top—unlike the standard stones, which are rounded. Pictured right is the front of the Daughters of Union Veterans memorial. Over 1,000 Union soldiers are buried in Jefferson Barracks. (Both, Connie Nisinger.)

Eric Knight (1897–1943), born in Yorkshire, England, moved to the United States after his divorced mother married an American. An author, film critic, and screenwriter, Knight wrote the 1940 novel *Lassie Come-Home*. The inset was taken on New Years Day in 1943. Two weeks later, on January 14, Major Knight and his crew died when their plane crashed in Dutch Guiana. The larger photograph was taken about 1995 at the crew's memorial in the cemetery. Pictured, left to right, are Knight's three daughters—Betty Knight Myers, Winifred Knight Mewborn, and Jennie Knight Moore. (Inset, Sylvia Salmi; larger image, Knight Family Archives.)

The national cemetery permits burial of both military personnel and spouses. Both are now buried on the front side of the tombstone, with the service person's information there. A spouse's information is on the back. Earlier practice in the cemetery provided for separate grave sites. John Gasparotti (1895–1959) was a World War I corporal. His wife, Elizabeth Seifert (1897–1983), a native Missourian, wrote over 80 romance novels during her career. They were usually set in the medical world. She was a top-selling writer in England as well. (Both, Connie Nisinger.)

During World War II, Jefferson Barracks drew two names at random from the list of enlisted men who had already died in the war and were buried in the cemetery. These men both had roads on the complex renamed after them. One of them, Donald Daniel Danner (1926–1943), was only 17 years old when killed in action on November 24, 1943. A native of South St. Louis, Danner was in the service about 18 months when his ship, the USS *Liscome Bay*, was sunk. (Connie Nisinger.)

Seven prisoners of war died during their imprisonment at Jefferson Barracks during World War II. The five Italians were Cesare Binetti, Nicola DiSalvo, Alfredo Ossemer, Cirolamo Pugliesi, and Talete Vivaldi. The two Germans buried there are Gustave Pfarrerr and Max Suemnick. (Connie Nisinger.)

The national cemetery has many mass graves. (Connie Nisinger.)

This area of the cemetery is known by some as the Circle because of the space void of graves in front of the flagpole. This area is near the original cemetery entrance. Near this space are the graves of both Michael Blassie and John F. Buck. (LOC, HABSMO 1938-14.)

Michael Blassie (1948–1972) was a young St. Louisan who served in the Vietnam War. He graduated from the US Air Force Academy in 1970. A first lieutenant, Blassie was piloting an A-378 Dragonfly when it was shot down near An Loc. His remains were buried in Arlington National Cemetery in the Tomb of the Unknowns. Later, his family requested permission to have the body exhumed. When it was granted, DNA tests proved the remains were those of Blassie. He was returned to St. Louis for burial in Jefferson Barracks. (Both, Connie Nisinger.)

The memorial here commends the Vietnam Khe Sanh veterans. (Art Schuermann.)

John F. "Jack" Buck (1924–2002) gained world renown as the voice of the St. Louis baseball Cardinals. Starting his career with broadcasts for football, his famous run with the baseball team started in 1954. He served nearly five decades broadcasting the Cardinals. Buck was a Hall of Fame broadcaster and has a star on the St. Louis Walk of Fame. His bronze statue, right, was draped in black following his death in 2002. (Both, St. Louis Cardinals Media Relations.)

Buck, a World War II Army corporal, was with K Company, 47th Regiment, 9th Infantry. He received a Purple Heart for wounds incurred on March 15, 1945, while facing the enemy marching in Germany over the bridge at Remagen. (Left, Art Schuermann; right, Connie Nisinger.)

Glenn C. Scott (1925–2009) was a private in the US Marine Corps in World War II. He received a Marksman Rifle badge and a Purple Heart. He earned a Bronze Star for heroic services in Iwo Jima on February 24, 1945. He, like most of the men, was a citizen soldier. And, like most following the war, he transitioned back to civilian life. Daily, nearly 1,000 American–World War II veterans pass away. (Barbara and Mary Scott.)

Just as the Spanish-American cannon stands sentinel elsewhere on the installation, the entrance to the national cemetery serves as a reminder to the country and the world of American history. The entrance stands tall, assuring the patriots who remain forever interred within the cemetery's gates that their efforts, acts, and sacrifices were not in vain and will not be forgotten (Marc Kollbaum.)

The sound of "Taps" drifts through the morning haze over the Jefferson Barracks National Cemetery time and time again. (Photograph by Virginia Todd.)

www.arcadiapublishing.com

Discover books about the town where you grew up, the cities where your friends and families live, the town where your parents met, or even that retirement spot you've been dreaming about. Our Web site provides history lovers with exclusive deals, advanced notification about new titles, e-mail alerts of author events, and much more.

MADE IN THE USA

Arcadia Publishing, the leading local history publisher in the United States, is committed to making history accessible and meaningful through publishing books that celebrate and preserve the heritage of America's people and places. Consistent with our mission to preserve history on a local level, this book was printed in South Carolina on American-made paper and manufactured entirely in the United States.

This book carries the accredited Forest Stewardship Council (FSC) label and is printed on 100 percent FSC-certified paper. Products carrying the FSC label are independently certified to assure consumers that they come from forests that are managed to meet the social, economic, and ecological needs of present and future generations.

FSC
Mixed Sources
Product group from well-managed forests and other controlled sources

Cert no. SW-COC-001530
www.fsc.org
© 1996 Forest Stewardship Council

Find Your Place in History.